Refugee Resettlement in the U.S.

Refugee Resettlement in the U.S.

First Edition

Shyam K. Sriram, Ph.D.

Canisius University

cognella®
SAN DIEGO

Bassim Hamadeh, CEO and Publisher
Craig Lincoln, Project Editor
Susana Christie, Senior Developmental Editor
Samantha Hansen, Production Editor
Jess Estrella, Senior Graphic Designer
Laura Duncan, Licensing Coordinator
Stephanie Adams, Senior Marketing Program Manager
Natalie Piccotti, Director of Marketing
Kassie Graves, Senior Vice President, Editorial

Printed in the United States of America.

320 South Cedros Ave., Ste. 400, Solana Beach, CA 92075

This textbook is dedicated to

John H. Siler (1947–2022)

Friend, father, public servant, educator, and soldier.

"All the times that I've cried/Keeping all the things I knew inside."—Cat Stevens

Contents

Acknowledgments   ix

Chapter 1   Refugee Resettlement Becomes Political   1

Chapter 2   The Holocaust, the United Nations, and Policy   15

Chapter 3   Immigration and Naturalization   27

Chapter 4   A Comparative Look at Immigration   41

Chapter 5   Federalism and State Policies   59

Chapter 6   American Support for Refugees   73

Chapter 7   Current Challenges to Resettlement and Integration (with Cathryn Bennett)   89

Acknowledgments

First and foremost, I testify there is no One worthy of worship except Allah (SWT), and Muhammad (SAW) is His final messenger. I remain eternally grateful to Dr. Syed Rashid Naim and Jamie Solesbee for introducing me to Islam in 2006, which opened the doors to an amazing journey. Jazak Allah Khair, may God reward you for the good that you do.

Second, I want to thank my beloved wife, Lizette, and our children, Naima, Elias, and Adonis, who have completed me in ways I never knew till I became their stepdad. The template for being a loving parent was established by my parents, Drs. Usha and Krishnan Sriram; my maternal grandparents, Vasantha and Jayaraman; and my late paternal grandparents, Janaki and Dr. P. Krishnan, whose marital devotion continues to inspire. I also want to thank my sister, Dr. Veena Sriram, her husband, Rohit, and my wonderful nieces, Zoya and Maya, for loving me wholly.

Third, I want to acknowledge my colleagues at Canisius University, who supported my vision, research, and teaching agenda on refugee resettlement and American politics. Paola Fajardo-Heyward, Kevin Hardwick, Girish Shambu, Bennie Williams, Fatima Rodriguez-Johnson, Julie Gibert, Aimee Larson, David Devereux, Richard Reitsma, John Kryder, Matt Kochan, Richard Bailey, Anita Butera, Jonathan Lawrence, and Erin Robinson are a great Buffalo family. A special thanks goes to Dean Tom Chambers, whose 2023 Summer Research Grant gave me the distraction-free time to focus on writing and complete the manuscript on time.

Last, this whole journey started in earnest in 2022 when I received an email from Angela Schultz at Cognella Academic Publishing soliciting textbook ideas. A phone conversation turned into a contract and a wonderful relationship over the last two years with a set of editors and production assistants who exceeded my expectations. A huge thanks to Susana Christie, Craig Lincoln, Rachel Kahn, Jess Estrella, Monica O'Keefe, Sannie Kirschner, and Samantha Hansen for their professionalism.

CHAPTER 1

Refugee Resettlement Becomes Political

Opening Vignette

November 15, 2015, could have been a fall day like any other in Paris, France, but it became one of the bloodiest the city and country had experienced since the conclusion of World War II seventy years earlier. The violence jarred "Paris and its very essence … under siege. A series of six coordinated attacks across Paris cut deep into the heart of Parisian existence."[1] President François Hollande declared a national state of emergency and President Barack Obama said, "Once again, we've seen an outrageous attempt to terrorize innocent civilians. This is an attack not just on Paris, it's an attack not just on the people of France, but this is an attack on all of humanity and the universal values that we share."[2]

Donald Trump, then a presidential candidate, tweeted on November 13, 2015, "My prayers are with the victims and hostages in the horrible Paris attacks. May God be with you all."[3] However, by November 14th, his messaging shifted focus. At 1:39 pm, he tweeted, "President Obama said 'ISIL continues to shrink' in an interview just hours before the horrible attack in Paris. He is just so bad! CHANGE." This was followed by "We need much tougher, much smarter leadership—and we need it NOW!" a few minutes later.[4]

QR Code 1.1

1. France24. 2015. "November 2015 Attacks: A Timeline of the Night That Shook the French Capital." https://www.france24.com/en/france/20210908-paris-november-2015-attacks-a-timeline-of-the-night-that-shook-the-city

2. Barack H. Obama. 2015. "President Obama Offers a Statement on the Attacks in Paris." *The White House*, November 13. https://obamawhitehouse.archives.gov/blog/2015/11/13/watch-president-obamas-statement-attacks-paris

3. Donald J. Trump. 2015. "Tweets of November 13, 2015." Online by Gerhard Peters and John T. Woolley, The American Presidency Project. https://www.presidency.ucsb.edu/node/346241

4. Donald J. Trump. 2015. "Tweets of November 14, 2015." Online by Gerhard Peters and John T. Woolley, The American Presidency Project. https://www.presidency.ucsb.edu/node/346242

That day at a rally in Beaumont, Texas, Trump referenced initial evidence that one of the terrorists in Paris had come into France with a Syrian passport: "And our president wants to take in 250,000 from Syria ... We all have heart, and we all want people taken care of and all of that, but with the problems our country has—to take in 250,000 people, some of whom are going to have problems, big problems is just insane. You have to be insane."[5]

Introduction to the Chapter

While the United States has accepted people fleeing political and religious persecution, the term refugee would not be applied until after the Holocaust and the efforts of the United Nations (which will be discussed more in subsequent chapters). A **refugee** is anyone, according to Article 1A (2) of the **1951 United Nations Convention on the Status of Refugees**, who

> owing to well-founded fear of persecution for reasons of race, religion, nationality, membership of a particular social group or political opinion, is outside the country of his nationality and is unable or, owing to such fear, is unwilling to avail himself of the protection of that country; or who, not having a nationality and being outside the country of his former habitual residence as a result of such events, is unable or, owing to such fear, is unwilling to return to it"[6]

In simpler language, a refugee is a person (including a child) who faces punishment or abuse based on their race, religion, politics, or nationality in their home country and does not feel like their government is protecting them. However, as you will learn in this textbook, the definition of a refugee is much more complex, nuanced, and dated; it has not caught up with recent global politics and international challenges.

> - Total Number of Refugees Admitted to the U.S. between 1975 and 2023: 3,574,352
> - Highest Single Year for Refugee Admissions: 1980 (207,116)
> - Lowest Single Year for Refugee Admissions: 2021 (11,411)
> - President With the Highest Admissions Total: Bill Clinton (715,046 in eight years)
> - President With the Highest Per Year Average: George H. W. Bush (118,764)

The Question: What do you notice about the difference between the political rhetoric and the actual numbers shown here? Why do you think this discrepancy exists?

---

5. Jenna Johnson. 2015. "Conservative Suspicions of Refugees Grow in Wake of Paris Attacks." *The Washington Post*, November 15. https://www.washingtonpost.com/politics/conservative-suspicions-of-refugees-grow-in-wake-of-paris-attacks/2015/11/15/ed553664-8baa-11e5-acff-673ae92ddd2b_story.html

6. U.N. High Commissioner for Refugees (UNHCR). 2011. "The 1951 Convention Relating to the Status of Refugees and its 1967 Protocol." https://www.refworld.org/docid/4ec4a7f02.html

Learning Objectives

Reading this chapter will enable readers to:

- **understand** the history of refugee resettlement in historical context in the United States.
- **interpret** the factors that lead to presidents responding to refugees differently.
- **identify** the timeframe when political rhetoric changed about refugees.

Understanding the History of Refugee Resettlement

The 2011 **Arab Spring**, a series of citizen-led revolts against Middle Eastern governments, resulted in an all-out civil war in Syria. By 2015, over 4 million Syrians were displaced outside the country and almost 8 million inside due to the wide-scale violence and abuse of Bashir Al-Assad, the Syrian president.[7] By the end of 2015, Europe would face its biggest humanitarian crisis since the Holocaust as over a million Syrians sought **asylum** —political protection—in Europe and then the United States.

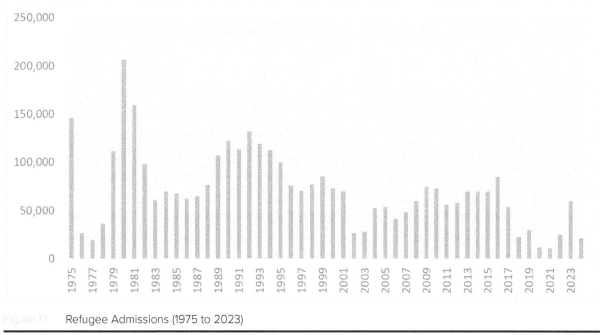

Figure 1.1   Refugee Admissions (1975 to 2023)

Data Source: https://www.wrapsnet.org/admissions-and-arrivals

Yet, despite the creation of an international standard, American foreign and domestic policy did not fall in line with global refugee law until the passage of the **1980 Refugee Act.** The U.S. Government started officially tracking refugee admissions in 1975, and we can see right away that the number has oscillated and jumped up and down

---

7. Wendy Pearlman. 2016. "Narratives of Fear in Syria." *Perspectives on Politics*, 14 (1): 21–37, p. 21.

wildly since then. The initial spike gave way to a huge fall, which slowly regained steam and skyrocketed in 1979 and 1980. As we talk about later in the book, multiple factors affected a decline in refugee admissions under President Reagan (including falling public opinion), but refugee admissions grew through the late 1980s and early 1990s also owing to the disintegration of the Soviet Union, the fall of the Berlin Wall, the Rwandan Genocide, the Yugoslavia Civil War, and other major events.

The 1980 Refugee Act[8]

- Legislation created after the Vietnam War to codify or clarify state and federal refugee policies.
- Passed by both chambers of Congress in 1979, and signed into law by President Jimmy Carter on March 17, 1980.[9]
- Lead sponsor in the U.S. Senate was Edward Kennedy (D-Massachusetts) and lead sponsor in the U.S. House of Representatives was Hamilton Fish Jr. (R-New York).
- The law established the Federal Office of Refugee Resettlement and also set the yearly refugee ceiling at 50,000.
- It also rectified the federal definition of a refugee so it was in line with that of the United Nations.

But the **September 11, 2001**, terrorist attacks in New York, Pennsylvania, and Virginia halted refugee admissions as domestic tensions rose surrounding immigrants and refugees, particularly from the Middle East, but also Pakistan and other Muslim-majority countries. The refugee numbers rebounded through the 2000s and hit a decades-long high by the end of President Barack Obama's second term before dropping precipitously during President Trump's administration. While there was an expectation that President Biden would revive the resettlement program to Obama-era numbers, most scholars and experts see Biden's attempts as falling far below what was expected from him after his 2021 inauguration, and his policies have been criticized by Republicans and Democrats.[10]

8. https://www.govinfo.gov/content/pkg/STATUTE-94/pdf/STATUTE-94-Pg102.pdf
9. National Archives Foundation. 2024. "Refugee Act of 1980." https://www.archivesfoundation.org/documents/refugee-act-1980/
10. Carroll, Conn. 2023. "The Intellectual Roots of Biden's Border Failure." *Washington Examiner*, December 22. https://www.washingtonexaminer.com/opinion/2670814/the-intellectual-roots-of-bidens-border-failure/. Michael D. Shear, Hamed Aleaziz, and Zolan Kanno-Youngs. 2024. "How the Border Crisis Shattered Biden's Immigration Hopes." The New York Times, January 30. https://www.nytimes.com/2024/01/30/us/politics/biden-border-crisis-immigration.html

Why Do Presidents Have Different Views About Refugees?

Presidents have several responsibilities and wear a lot of different hats. These include their roles as commander in chief of the armed forces, head of state, head of government, unofficial leader of their political party, chief diplomat, and chief executive of the federal government. Presidents are also influenced by campaign promises, public opinion, domestic events, and global leaders and crises.

For example, the United States was involved in a drawn-out, decades-long conflict with the former Union of Soviet Socialist Republics (USSR), or Soviet Union, that began post-World War II and ramped up in the late 1940s and early 1950s.[11] The **Cold War**, as it was known, was not only an ideological campaign that pitted the United States and its allies against the Soviet Union and its allies but also spurred several proxy wars where the USA and USSR did not fight each other directly but took sides in other conflicts. Examples include the Korean War and the Vietnam War.

Presidents during this time were often challenged to accept refugees and political immigrants fleeing countries where they faced persecution for holding anti-Soviet or anti-Communist beliefs. The 1956 Hungarian Revolution was waged by the people of Hungary against the Soviet Union, which had occupied their country since 1945. Of the 200,000 Hungarians who fled the country, the United States, under President Dwight D. Eisenhower, accepted 38,000.[12] A wave of Chinese refugees was also accepted in the United States between 1948 and 1966, many of them intellectuals and scholars. According to historian Madeline Hsu, "The Department of State and the executive branch used refugee admissions to foster stronger overseas alliances and promote America's image as a democratic society."[13] Some of the first Chinese refugees came under the 1948 Displaced Persons Act, the 1952 McCarran Walter Act, and the Refugee Relief Act of 1953.[14]

What the 1980 Refugee Act did was create a unified federal-state policy that allowed a more even annual response to refugees compared to past legislation passed every few years by Congress to help people displaced by various crises. However, as we learn toward the end of this textbook, Americans have not always been supportive of accepting refugees despite the urgent need and humanitarian crises.

After Congress passed the 1980 Refugee Act, every president has set a yearly **refugee ceiling,** or maximum number of refugees that could be accepted, of at least 50,000 people minimum per year. Most presidents exceeded the refugee ceiling but had never lowered it until President Trump took office. While campaigning for office in 2015 and 2016, Trump used refugees from Syria as an example of the kind of people he believed were not good for the country, conflating Muslims in Syria with terrorist organizations like ISIS, Al-Qaeda, and the Taliban.

11. https://www.jfklibrary.org/learn/about-jfk/jfk-in-history/the-cold-war

12. Peter Pastor. 2016. "The American Reception and Settlement of Hungarian Refugees in 1956–1957." *e-Journal of the American Hungarian Educators Association*, 9: 197–205.

13. Madeline Hsu. 2012. "The Disappearance of America's Cold War Chinese Refugees, 1948–1966." *Journal of American Ethnic History*, 31 (4): 12–33, p. 14.

14. Ibid, p. 16.

Figure 1.2   Displaced Vietnamese on a U.S. aircraft carrier.

The end of the **Vietnam War** resulted in one of the largest exoduses ever of displaced people, but it also created a lot of domestic pressure in the United States. Even though our country took in a large number of people from Southeast Asia, there was a lot of opposition within the United States from various local and state governments who felt that government systems—housing, education, employment, welfare, etc.—had not been established to deal with a large influx of refugees. Over 125,000 refugees from Vietnam were resettled in 1975 alone.[15] According to the International Rescue Committee, "During the 20 years after the fall of Saigon, some two million people poured out of Vietnam, Laos and Cambodia. By 1992, more than a million had been admitted to the U.S."[16]

15. Laura Harjanto, and Jeanne Batalova. 2021. "Vietnamese Immigrants in the United States." Migration Policy Center (Migration Information Source). October 15. https://www.migrationpolicy.org/article/vietnamese-immigrants-united-states

16. IRC. 2016. "The Largest Refugee Resettlement Effort in American History." International Rescue Committee (Rescue Timeline—1975), July 28. https://www.rescue.org/article/largest-refugee-resettlement-effort-american-history

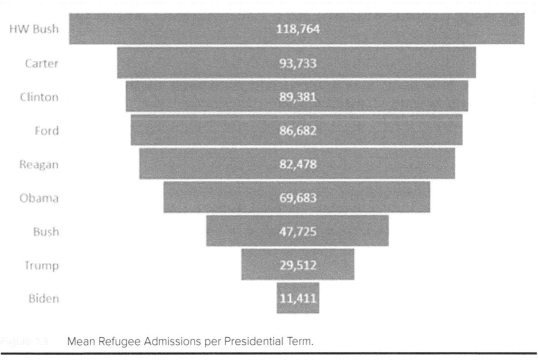

Figure 1.3   Mean Refugee Admissions per Presidential Term.

Data Source: https://www.wrapsnet.org/documents/
Refugee%20Admissions%20by%20Region%20since%201975%20as%20of%2030%20Sep%202021.pdf

Figure 1.3 illustrates a fact that many people might find surprising: based on the average number of refugee admissions per year, President George H. W. Bush was the most "generous" head of state this country has ever seen.[17] During his four years in office (January 1989 to January 1993), the United States welcomed 475,056 refugees, or an average of 118,764 per year. However, if we look at the total number of refugee admissions over a presidential term, President Clinton's 715,046 admitted over eight years would be the highest (January 1993 to January 2001). Trump's tenure as president was also unusual because it was a stark change from past Republican presidents who were, on average, more welcoming of refugees than their Democratic peers.[18]

17. The data on President Biden captures January 2021 to February 2024. President Gerald Ford was only in office for two and a half years after the resignation of President Richard Nixon in 1974.
18. Shyam K. Sriram. 2019. "Donald Trump's New Refugee Admissions Cap Is a Record Low, and a Departure for a Republican President." United States Politics and Policy Blog (London School of Economics), October 2. https://blogs.lse.ac.uk/usappblog/2019/10/02/donald-trumps-new-refugee-admissions-cap-is-a-record-low-and-a-departure-for-a-republican-president/

Scapegoating Syrians and the 2016 Presidential Campaign

Since 2015, how many acts of terrorism have been attributed to Syrian refugees in the United States?

ZERO

After Donald Trump's November 15, 2015, Texas rally, his tweets became even more intense:

"When will President Obama issue the words RADICAL ISLAMIC TERRORISM? He can't say it, and unless he will, the problem will not be solved!" (November 15, 2015)[19]

"Refugees from Syria are now pouring into our great country. Who knows who they are—some could be ISIS. Is our president insane?" (November 17, 2015)[20]

"13 Syrian refugees were caught trying to get into the U.S. through the Southern Border. How many made it? WE NEED THE WALL!" (November 22, 2015)[21]

"Crooked Hillary wants a radical 500% increase in Syrian refugees. We can't allow this. Time to get smart and protect America!" (May 22, 2016)[22]

"CLINTON REFUGEE PLAN COULD BRING IN 620,000 REFUGEES IN FIRST TERM AT LIFETIME COST OF OVER $400 BILLION." (August 15, 2016)[23]

Trump made the ISIS attacks in Paris a story, not about resilience but one of blame. His rhetoric blamed open-border policies in France but made the attacks secondary to the real issue at hand, in his opinion: President Obama's

19. Donald J. Trump. 2015. "Tweets of November 15, 2015." Online by Gerhard Peters and John T. Woolley, The American Presidency Project. https://www.presidency.ucsb.edu/node/346243

20. Donald J. Trump. 2015. "Tweets of November 17, 2015." Online by Gerhard Peters and John T. Woolley, The American Presidency Project. https://www.presidency.ucsb.edu/node/346245

21. Donald J. Trump. 2015. "Tweets of November 22, 2015." Online by Gerhard Peters and John T. Woolley, The American Presidency Project. https://www.presidency.ucsb.edu/node/346250

22. Donald J. Trump. 2016. "Tweets of May 22, 2016." Online by Gerhard Peters and John T. Woolley, The American Presidency Project. https://www.presidency.ucsb.edu/node/346463

23. Donald J. Trump. 2016. "Tweets of August 15, 2016." Online by Gerhard Peters and John T. Woolley, The American Presidency Project. https://www.presidency.ucsb.edu/node/346151.

apparently similar approach in the United States. By conflating French and American policies, Trump quickly engaged the public on a policy issue that had quietly existed under the radar: refugee admissions and resettlement.

Almost overnight, the story in the United States became about how Paris might be repeated here if the government did not vet or screen refugees better. Some politicians went so far as to claim that Christian refugees were acceptable but not Muslim ones. Senator Ted Cruz asked Muslim-majority countries to take Syrian Muslims and told the audience at a South Carolina middle school that "There is no meaningful risk of Christians committing acts of terror."[24]

Religion was confused with race, ethnicity, and country of origin in a pattern that had eerily similarities to the days, weeks, and months after 9/11 when anyone who "looked Muslim" became guilty by association. **Islamophobia** in the United States became all too real again. Muslim Americans suffered physical, emotional, and economic attacks but so did other Americans who were dragged into the post-9/11 ignorance and confusion. Sikh men, who wear turbans to cover their long hair and who often grow long beards, were beaten and killed for looking like the Taliban. There were 300 anti-Sikh attacks across the country in just the first month after 9/11.[25]

Figure 1.4   A Sikh American man at a 2011 Independence Day Parade in Washington, D.C.

Copyright © by S. Pakhrin (CC BY 2.0) at https://commons.wikimedia.org/wiki/ File:Independence_day_Parade_2011_DC_-_0oe_(5905888725).jpg.

24. Amy Davidson Sorkin. 2015. "Ted Cruz's Religious Test for Syrian Refugees." *The New Yorker*, November 16. https://www.newyorker.com/news/ amy-davidson/ted-cruzs-religious-test-for-syrian-refugees

25. The Sikh Coalition. 2022. "Fact Sheet on Post-9/11 Discrimination and Violence Against Sikh Americans." https://www.sikhcoalition.org/ images/documents/fact%20sheet%20on%20hate%20against%20sikhs%20in%20america%20post%209-11%201.pdf

Islamophobia

- Islamophobia is often defined as an irrational fear and/or hatred of Muslims and the religion of Islam.
- Islamophobia in the United States and the public perception of Muslims is often linked to 9/11 and the subsequent wars in Iraq and Afghanistan.
- A key feature of American Islamophobia is that Islam became racialized, i.e., even though American Muslims represent dozens of ethnicities, races, and countries of origin; black and brown people were often targeted more for "looking Muslim."
- Post-9/11 Islamophobia is also characterized by the belief that Islam is tied to criminality. According to anthropologist Junaid Rana, "The figures of the terrorist and the migrant are woven together in the figure of 'the Muslim' as a racial type."[26]

Trump, Cruz, and other politicians and public figures made refugee resettlement political, a label that had not been applied since after the Vietnam War. What this means is that even though refugee resettlement is a type of public policy that is created by governments, it is often not scrutinized by the public and the people the way that, let's say, unemployment, often is discussed. Most Americans know little about who qualifies as a refugee; how refugees are different from immigrants; what is political asylum; the role of resettlement organizations; and which level of government is responsible for accepting, resettling, and aiding refugees (answer: all levels). This was one of the motivations behind writing this textbook—to help educators and students learn more about refugee resettlement in high school and college.

Even though Syrian refugees and asylum seekers were pre-emptively labeled terrorists—with no proof—most Americans started to believe that Syrian refugees were a threat to peace in the United States. Trump's tweets became more than just hyperbole or exaggeration; they became the foundation for anti-immigrant rhetoric across the country. One of the worst ways this happened was that for the first time in U.S. history, many governors publicly said their states would not accept refugees from Syria.[27] This also created a quagmire of legal questions: could states refuse the federal government's resettlement of refugees and refuse to collaborate? Was resettlement solely a national policy? Former Michigan Governor Rick Snyder said, "Michigan is a welcoming state and we are proud of our rich history of immigration … But our first priority is protecting the safety of our residents."[28] Paul LePage, then governor of Maine, said, "To bring Syrian refugees into our country without knowing who they are is to invite an attack on American soil just like the one we saw in Paris last week and in New York City on 9/11."[29] In a similar tone, Arizona Governor

26. Rana, Junaid. 2011. Terrifying Muslims: Race and Labor in the South Asian Diaspora. Durham, NC: Duke University Press, p. 5.
27. Jesse Byrnes. 2015. "More Than Half of U.S. Governors Oppose Refugee Resettlement." The Hill (National Security), November 17. https://thehill.com/policy/national-security/260388-more-than-half-of-us-governors-oppose-refugee-resettlement/
28. https://www.freep.com/story/news/local/michigan/2015/11/15/snyder-suspends-efforts-settle-syrian-refugees/75825736/
29. https://www.pressherald.com/2015/11/16/as-republican-governors-reject-syrian-refugees-lepage-not-as-forceful/.

Doug Ducey asked the federal government to "take into account the concerns and recommendations of the state of Arizona ... [and] the world remains at war with radical Islamic terrorists."[30]

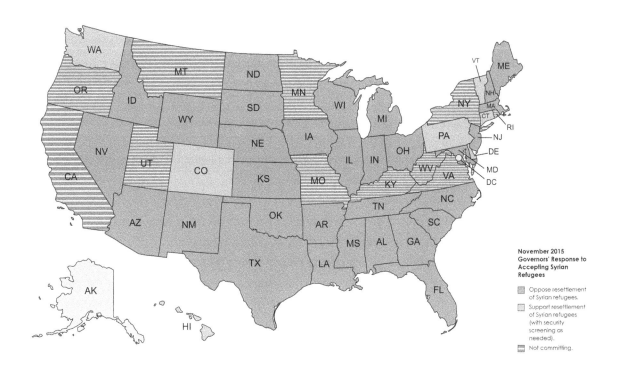

Figure 1.5   US Governors and Their Responses to Accepting Syrian Refugees in 2015.

Conclusion

While zero terrorist attacks would be attributed to Syrian refugees in the United States since 2015, the damage had been done to the public's understanding and acceptance of refugees broadly but specifically, those fleeing Bashir Al-Assad's murderous campaign in Syria. According to 2018 numbers, Turkey took on the greatest responsibility and accepted 3.6 million Syrian refugees. They were followed by Lebanon (944,000), Jordan (676,000), and Germany

30. https://azgovernor.gov/governor/news/2015/11/statement-governor-doug-ducey

(532,000).[31] In sharp, depressing contrast, the United States under President Barack Obama accepted only 12,623 Syrian refugees between October 2010 and August 2016.[32]

In one of his first acts as president, Donald Trump used Executive Order 13769 on February 1, 2017, to freeze the refugee ceiling and ordered the secretary of state to suspend the U.S. Refugee Admissions Program (USRAP) for 120 days.[33] The United States would only accept 3,024 Syrian refugees in 2017.[34] By politicizing refugee resettlement on the 2015 and 2016 campaign trail, Donald Trump rode the anti-immigration wave all the way to the White House and then embarked on a series of immigration- and refugee-related executive orders that the country has still not recovered from (and which will be discussed in subsequent chapters).

List of Key Takeaways

Review the list of bullet points below for a quick overview of the key ideas and information in this chapter:

- The United Nations defines a refugee as someone who is so afraid of their country of origin that they cannot return to that place because of a "well-founded fear of persecution for reasons of race, religion, nationality, membership of a particular social group or political opinion."
- The United States's definition of a refugee did not match that of the United Nations until the passage of the 1980 Refugee Act, a response to the large number of refugees accepted by the U.S. after the Vietnam War.
- Trump ran for office in 2015 and 2016 on an antirefugee platform and convinced the majority of governors to also oppose accepting Syrian refugees.
- Presidents typically accepted at least 50,000 refugees ever year—also known as the "refugee ceiling"—and would often raise the ceiling to accept more.
- President Donald Trump was the first president to lower the ceiling.
- Refugee admissions are affected by global crises, but each president has a lot of discretion when it comes to the number of people their administration wants to accept.

Chapter Review Questions

1. **Summarize** the most important features of the 1980 Refugee Act.
2. **Identify** the crisis that caused refugee admissions to dwindle in the early 2000s. Why were Americans hesitant to welcome refugees at that time?

31. https://www.pbs.org/wgbh/frontline/article/numbers-syrian-refugees-around-world
32. Bruno, Andorra. 2016. "Syrian Refugee Admissions and Resettlement in the United States: In Brief." Congressional Research Service, September 16 (Summary). https://sgp.fas.org/crs/homesec/R44277.pdf
33. https://www.federalregister.gov/documents/2017/02/01/2017-02281/protecting-the-nation-from-foreign-terrorist-entry-into-the-united-states
34. https://www.npr.org/sections/parallels/2018/04/12/602022877/the-u-s-has-welcomed-only-11-syrian-refugees-this-year

3. **Interpret** Figure 1.3: What kind of information can we glean from this graph?
    a. Democratic presidents are friendlier toward refugees compared to Republican presidents.
    b. There is a chronological decline in the number of refugees allowed by presidents.
    c. President George H. W. Bush accepted more refugees on average per year than any other president in history. (CORRECT)
    d. President Biden has accepted more refugees than President Trump.
4. **Explain** why President Eisenhower took in 38,000 refugees from Hungary.
5. **Interpret** this statement: "A key feature of American Islamophobia is that Islam became racialized."
6. **Describe** how Donald Trump's tweets introduced religion as a criteria for refugee admissions.

Critical Thinking Prompts

1. **Formulate** a new, twenty-first century definition of a refugee. What is missing from the United Nations's original criteria?
2. Did the United States have a responsibility to take in more Syrian refugees than we actually did? **Justify** your response.
3. Should states and governors be able to refuse refugees from any country the states deem as a threat (even if this conflicts with federal policy)? **Recommend** a policy position that incorporates states' rights and federalism.

CHAPTER 2

The Holocaust, the United Nations, and Policy

Opening Vignette

In 2011, a team of student filmmakers joined hands with a group of Holocaust survivors under the banner of a new project titled *Righteous Conversations*.[1] Their goal was to create intergenerational bonds and to keep the stories of the Holocaust alive. In response to the 2015 Syrian Refugee Crisis, the *Righteous Conversations Project* came together to engineer a new, short film about the need for empathy and understanding around the forced displacement of Syrians. The video, titled "Belonging," alternates between student and survivor voices and is a powerful visual document about the need to show compassion. The short film begins with one young filmmaker who says, "We are all human beings, looking for a home." He is followed by a survivor who responds to the gutting image of two-year-old Alan Kurdi, whose body washed to shore in Turkey: "Seeing the little child, lying, just brought tears to my eyes." Later in the video, another survivor firmly states, "We all need to know we have a safe place to be, a safe home, a safe environment." According to Samara Hutman, project co-founder,

> For them [Holocaust survivors], this is more than a problem that is unfolding on the other side of the planet. For them, it is a story with kinship to their own. They were children in Hitler's Europe. They hid, they feared, they were hungry and cold. They know what it means to wonder, "Does anyone in the world know I am here?" It is their own childhoods that shaped their compassion for this new wave of refugees.[2]

QR Code 2.1

1. http://righteousconversations.org/
2. Rachel Nusbaum. 2016. "Students and Holocaust Survivors Team Up for Refugee PSA." HIAS, February 22. https://www.hias.org/blog/students-and-holocaust-survivors-team-refugee-psa

Introduction to the Chapter

The story of refugee policy and resettlement is predicated on an understanding of **the Holocaust** and how Adolf Hitler's treatment of the Jewish people—and anyone who stood in his way—changed history. To dismiss the Holocaust in a study of refugee resettlement is historical revisionism; though eighty-years later, there are still people who shockingly deny the Holocaust happened at all, and often belong to "far-right, neo-Nazi, and white power groups."[3] As President Biden reaffirmed on April 22, 2022, Holocaust Remembrance Day (*Yom HaShoah*),

> We recognize that, just as the Holocaust was an act of pure antisemitism, so too Holocaust denial is a form of antisemitism … Efforts to minimize, distort, or blur who the Nazis were and the genocide they perpetrated are a form of Holocaust denial and, in addition to insulting both the victims and survivors of the Holocaust, spread antisemitism.[4]

- The Holocaust is defined as "the systematic, bureaucratic, state-sponsored persecution and murder of Jewish men, women, and children by the Nazi regime and its collaborators.
- Estimated number of Jewish victims of the Holocaust: 6 million.
- Estimated number of Soviet civilians and prisoners of war, non-Jewish Polish civilians, people with disabilities, LGBTQ individuals, political prisoners, Roma (Gypsies), criminals, and other victims of the Holocaust: Over 11 million.
- Estimated number of Jews who were killed at Auschwitz and its sub-camps: 1 million.

The destruction caused by the Holocaust and the attempted extermination of the Jewish people moved Raphael Lemkin, a Polish lawyer and scholar whose parents were murdered at Treblinka, to coin the phrase **genocide**. According to Lemkin, genocide was the "coordinated plan of different actions aiming at the destruction of essential foundations of the life of national groups, with the aim of annihilating the groups themselves."[5] Lemkin continued to pressure the United Nations to recognize genocide as the most severe of crimes, the attempt to destroy an entire people, and was singlehandedly responsible for the 1948 Convention on the Prevention and Punishment of the Crime of Genocide.[6] It is also important to mention that even before Lemkin's campaign of recognition related to the Holocaust, genocides were perpetrated by the United States, Canada, and European powers against Indigenous

---

3. Deborah Lipstadt. 2020. "Holocaust Denial: An Antisemitic Fantasy." *Modern Judaism*, 40 (1): 71–86, p. 73.
4. Joseph R. Biden. 2022. "Proclamation 10373 of April 22, 2022: Days of Remembrance of Victims of the Holocaust, 2022." Federal Register, 87 (81). https://www.govinfo.gov/content/pkg/FR-2022-04-27/pdf/2022-09132.pdf
5. https://www.hmd.org.uk/resource/raphael-lemkin/
6. UNHCR. 2017. "Lemkin, Raphael." https://www.unhcr.org/ceu/9486-lemkin-raphael.html

Americans (beginning in the fifteenth century), Germany against the Herero and Nama people (1904 and 1907),[7] and the Ottoman Empire against Armenians (1915–1923).[8]

Those who survived the brutality of Hitler's death camps, which were built all over Europe (**see Figure 2.1**), often had no homes to return to during and after the war: whole towns were wiped off the map. People fled around the world and were met with open and closed arms. One of the myths we tell ourselves now is that the world's leaders in the early twentieth century were hospitable and welcoming of the Jewish victims of the Holocaust, but the reality is far from it. There were a few countries who opened their borders, communities, and hearts to European Jews, but many places did not want these displaced peoples, including the United States (which we will discuss later). It was the intervention of the United Nations after World War II and the creation first, of the **United Nations High Commissioner for Refugees** (UNHCR) in 1950,[9] the Convention on the Status of Refugees in 1951, and later, conventions that laid the foundation for international humanitarian law, which is the focus of this chapter.

The Question: Why does hospitality seem to be selective? Don't all displaced people deserve the right to be accepted as guests in other countries?

Learning Objectives

Reading this chapter will enable readers to:

- **Demonstrate** knowledge of the Holocaust and early attempts for Jews to escape Europe.
- **Enumerate** the United Nations's requirements to be classified as a refugee.
- **Identify** areas where international law and policy must be updated for the current time.

7. World Without Genocide. 2023. "Genocide of the Herero and Nama." Mitchell Hamline School of Law. https://worldwithoutgenocide.org/genocides-and-conflicts/herero-and-nama.
8. Rouben Paul Adalian. 2024. "Armenian Genocide (1915–1923)." Armenian National Institute. https://www.armenian-genocide.org/genocide.html.
9. https://www.unhcr.org/en-us/history-of-unhcr.html

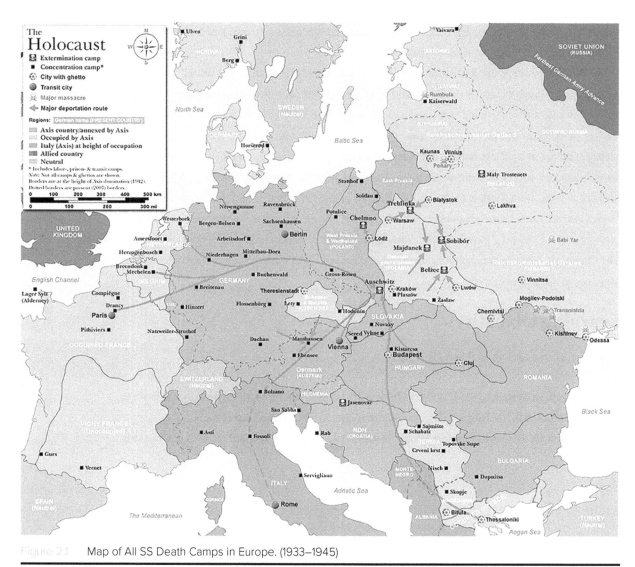

Figure 2.1   Map of All SS Death Camps in Europe. (1933–1945)

The Holocaust and Trying to Escape Europe

Germany's invasion of Poland on September 1, 1939, is widely accepted as the start of World War II. However, the beginnings of a comprehensive German attack on Jewish religious, cultural, financial, and physical well-being began as early as 1933 and Hitler's ascension to power. This is an important detail because the post-World War I landscape with the Treaty of Versailles and the League of Nations created the framework, which would later be used to aid Jewish refugees desperate to escape Germany and Austria well before the official beginning of the Second World War. In October 1933, the League of Nations created the position of High Commissioner for the Refugees from Germany and appointed an American professor, James G. McDonald, but was more symbolic with little power of enforcement: "Without the authority or resources of the League behind it, it had to find its own way and was left to sink or swim, while it tried as best it could to find a place for the refugees in countries that did not want them."[10] Indeed, within two years, McDonald would resign, "with little to show for his efforts, in despair, disappointment, frustration and sheer exhaustion over wrestling with international intransigence in the face of the refugees and Nazi barbarity towards its citizens."[11]

The March 1938 occupation of Austria (also known as the Anschluss)[12] and the November 1938 *Kristallnacht,* or the Night of Broken Glass, (**see Figure 2.2**), where thousands of businesses and synagogues were destroyed,[13] accelerated emigration out of Europe. Not only had the Nazis been planning a "Reichspogromnacht," or state-sponsored pogrom (mass violence), against German Jews for some time, but they used the event to retaliate for the assassination of Ernst Vom Rath, a German diplomat. Accordingly, "Vom Rath became an instant folk hero, and as always, the Jews retained their role as the 'eternal' enemy of the Germans."[14]

But there was still no globally accepted understanding of who or what constituted a refugee, how countries were supposed to help each other, and who or what would oversee all of this. Worse, however, was that despite widespread knowledge of what the Nazis were capable of and their singular focus to obliterate Jewish people and their identity, many countries were still reluctant to take in these political immigrants. The United States, for example, used its own 1924 Johnson-Reed Act to set country quotas that "were calculated to privilege 'desirable' immigrants from northern and western Europe. They limited immigrants considered less 'racially desirable,' including southern and eastern European Jews."[15] Eventually, the United States, under President Franklin D. Roosevelt, would accept 123,868 Jewish people to come here, but many more were not given the opportunity due to paperwork, administrative delays, and highly restrictive policies.[16]

The Great Depression also hung over the United States like a funereal fog, and most Americans were opposed to immigration and sharing what limited resources were available. (We will tackle public opinion toward refugees in detail in Chapter 6). A 1938 Roper/Fortune poll asked respondents, "What is your attitude toward allowing German, Austrian, and other political refugees to come into the United States?" and if immigration quotes should be raised. The tally was 67% were opposed, 23% were in favor, and 10% had no opinion.[17]

10. Greg Burgess. 2016. "Introduction." In The League of Nations and the Refugees from Nazi German. London: Bloomsbury Academic, 1–12, p. 2.

11. Ibid, p. 4.

12. United States Holocaust Memorial Museum. 2022. "Nazi Territorial Aggression: The Anschluss." Holocaust Encyclopedia: https://encyclopedia.ushmm.org/content/en/article/nazi-territorial-aggression-the-anschluss

13. https://www.pbs.org/wgbh/americanexperience/features/holocaust-kristallnacht/

14. Karen Sutton. 2022. "Kristallnacht: A Lethal Legacy of Legends and Lies." *The Detroit Jewish News* (Purely Commentary), November 18. https://thejewishnews.com/2022/11/18/purely-commentary-kristallnacht-a-lethal-legacy-of-legends-and-lies/

15. United States Holocaust Memorial Museum. 2022. "Immigration to the United States, 1933–1941." Holocaust Encyclopedia. https://encyclopedia.ushmm.org/content/en/article/immigration-to-the-united-states-1933-41

16. Ibid.

17. Fortune. Roper/Fortune Survey, May, 1938(survey question). USROPER.38-01.Q07. Roper Organization(producer). Cornell University, Ithaca, NY: Roper Center for Public Opinion Research, iPOLL [distributor].

Another highly publicized and deleterious event in 1939 involved the *St. Louis*, a ship carrying **just over 900 Jewish refugees,** that headed first to Cuba with the expectation that the Cuban government would accept them with open arms. The Museum of Jewish Heritage described the scene on the ship as "festive" and many "giddy with a sense of relief."[18] Soon, however, "The mood changed dramatically when, fourteen days later, the ship entered Cuban territorial waters. To the consternation of the passengers, Cuban officials refused to come aboard to begin the immigration process." Only 22 Jews were allowed to disembark and then the ship's passengers, now overcome with shock and dread, started to think that the United States would accept them (but that would not happen either).[19]

18. Museum of Jewish Heritage—A Living Memorial to the Holocaust. 2022. "The Voyage of the St. Louis." Jewish Life, May 5. https://mjhnyc.org/
    blog/the-voyage-of-the-st-louis/
19. Ibid.

Figure 2.3   Passengers on board the *S.S. St. Louis*, 1939. This photo was taken when the ship reached Antwerp, Belgium, and the passengers were given the joyous news that they would be given sanctuary. Their celebration was short-lived; in 1940, Germany successfully invaded and occupied Belgium. Many of the refugees, possibly including some pictured here, subsequently perished under the Nazi regime.

American Jewish Joint Distribution Committee, "Jewish Passengers on the Deck of the St. Louis (1939)," https://photos.yadvashem.org/photo-details.html?language=en&item_id=32054&ind=15. Copyright © 1939 by Yad Vashem.

Though some Jewish organizations like the JDC tried to cooperate with governments in the Americas,[20] no country would take the Jewish refugees in as people urgently needing asylum. After 12 days on the high seas and docked near Cuba and the United States, the ship headed back to Europe. While some passengers were eventually accepted by a few countries, many returned to their original homes and subsequently died in the Holocaust.

The 1951 Refugee Convention

Imagine this scene. Adolf Hitler has committed suicide. Germany has surrendered, and unbelievably, finally, the war in Europe is over. You have been separated from your parents and are in an orphanage in Denmark. The last time you saw family was in your village in Poland, which no longer exists. Some of your siblings have escaped to British Palestine, and some aunts and uncles (and maybe even your parents) survived Sobibor, a death camp, and are now living together in a bombed-out building in Czechoslovakia. Where do you go? Whom do you trust?

20. JDC. 2022. "The Story of the S.S. St. Louis." JDC Archives. https://archives.jdc.org/topic-guides/the-story-of-the-s-s-st-louis/

This scenario was the reality for millions of men, women, and children in the weeks, months, and years after the "end" of World War II. While combat operations may have ceased, the lived experiences of millions of displaced people tell a different story. Europe was overwhelmed by the sheer mass of humanity whose homes had been destroyed and who still faced the threats of violence and antisemitism if they dared return to their places of origin. Over 23 million people were displaced in Germany alone, including soldiers, civilians, death and labor camp survivors, unaccompanied children, and many more.[21]

Still reeling from the failures of the League of Nations post-World War I, the newly created United Nations was established after the San Francisco Conference between May and June 1945 and whose charter was officially ratified on October 24, 1945.[22] Even before the UN was officially established, Allied powers created the United Nations Rehabilitation and Repatriation Administration (UNRRA) whose sole purpose was to help displaced people in Europe reconnect with family members and loved ones and return home. But the task was too enormous and complex, and even by 1946, there were over a million displaced people still living in special postwar camps.[23] The International Refugee Organization was also created by the U.N. in 1946 and intended to replace the UNRRA but with a slightly different purpose: "to give those who refused to return home to Communist countries the option of resettlement in the West."[24] But there was still no official and globally accepted understanding of who constituted a refugee and what responsibilities lay for countries outside of Europe who saw their identity now as more accepting of displaced people (even if they had opposed refugee resettlement during the war). This would only change with the 1951 Refugee Convention.

The 1948 Universal Declaration of Human Rights laid the groundwork and created global standards for the subsequent Refugee Convention and every other universal statement on human rights and their protections.[25] This would become imperative with the 1951 Convention Relating to the Status of Refugees (usually referred to as "the Convention" or "the Refugee Convention") and the 1967 Protocol on the Status of Refugees, which expanded the initial European-refugee mandate and applied the definition of refugee to displaced people everywhere.

Even before the end of the Second World War, "persecution as a criterion for refugee status already existed … tacitly and implicitly underpinning refugee definition adopted by the League of Nations and subsequent bodies in the postwar period."[26] However, it became codified in the 1951 Convention with the formal definition of a refugee in Article 1, Section A (2) as a person who,

> owing to well-founded fear of being persecuted for reasons of race, religion, nationality, membership of a particular social group or political opinion, is outside the country of his nationality and is unable or, owing to such fear, is unwilling to avail himself of the protection

21. Ruth Balint. 2021. Destination Elsewhere: Displaced Persons and Their Quest to Leave Postwar Europe. Ithaca, NY: Cornell University Press, p. 1.
22. United Nations. 2022. "Milestones in UN History, 1941–1950." https://www.un.org/en/about-us/history-of-the-un/1941-1950
23. Balint (2021, 3).
24. Ibid, p. 4.
25. Shayam Sriram. 2020. "Civil Rights." In Introduction to Political Science, eds. Mark Carl Rom, Masaki Hidaka, and Rachel Bzostek Walker. OpenStax, p. 201–234.
26. Balint (2021, p. 25).

of that country; or who, not having a nationality and being outside the country of his former habitual residence as a result of such events, is unable or, owing to such fear, is unwilling to return to it.[27]

One way to think about this definition is the implication that a state or country does not see one of its own citizens as guaranteeing the same protection and civil rights it offers another. So, the refugee must leave and cannot return home; their "refugehood" is a journey "from one sovereign state into the power and jurisdiction of another."[28] The Convention also specified who would not be protected, including crimes against humanity, war crimes, acts that went against the spirit of the United Nations. Additionally, the Convention clearly states that refugees must follow the rules of the country that accepts them and that "Contracting States" or the countries who adhere to the 1951 Refugee Convention must not discriminate against refugees and must afford refugees the same freedom of religion as they would to their own citizens.

Challenges to Refugee Law

The biggest challenge to international refugee law is the lack of common vision from U.N. member countries, which directly leads to frustrating issues of compliance. It is often difficult for people outside of the legal arena to understand *why* there is a lack of compliance when sovereign countries willingly agree to join international bodies like the United Nations but then balk at collective decisions that affect all countries and some more than others. This happened in the United States, too, when the Senate did not ratify the 1948 Genocide Convention … until 1988. As the *Washington Post* noted in an editorial, "Ninety-six nations have ratified this treaty, which grew out of the horrors of the Holocaust. This country has stalled for 40 years in accepting a commitment that is in every way consistent with American ideals. The Senate should cast its final vote on the merits of the bill without a distracting dispute on capital punishment."[29]

A more recent example of sovereign resistance to the 1951 Refugee Convention is Lebanon, which accepts and resettles millions of refugees but still refuses to be an official signatory to the Refugee Convention. While the Middle East and Arab states are often noted for their "non-commitment to international refugee law," Lebanon is recognized as being highly supportive of the rights of displaced peoples historically.[30] And yet, as Maja Janmyr has researched, the Lebanese Constitution does not allow any foreigners to become permanent residents or citizens; in fact, the Lebanon Crisis Response Plan (LCRP) actually states "Lebanon is neither a country of asylum, nor a final destination for refugees, let alone a country of resettlement."[31] So, Lebanon purposively maintains its own right to follow international norms but carries out its own domestic understanding of who qualifies as a refugee.

27. UNHCR. 2021. Convention and Protocol Relating to the Status of Refugees (Chapter 1), p. 14.

28. Charlotte Lülf. 2019. Conflict Displacement and Legal Protection: Understanding Asylum, Human Rights and Refugee Law. London: Routledge, p. 6.

29. The Editorial Board. 1988. "Completing the Genocide Treaty." *The Washington Post*, April 26. https://www.washingtonpost.com/archive/opinions/1988/04/26/completing-the-genocide-treaty/5e13e679-6e57-49d9-bf39-841040219c14/

30. Maja Janmyr. 2017. "No Country of Asylum: Legitimizing Lebanon's Rejection of the 1951 Refugee Convention." International Journal of Refugee Law, 29 (3): 438–465, p. 439.

31. Ibid, p. 440.

One perspective on the challenge of compliance is that there is too little enforcement of international law; who punishes whom, what should penalties be, can they be objective, and what happens when countries neither accept the punishment nor care about being punished in the first place?[32] For example, the UNHCR, which we have discussed in several places throughout this chapter, is the refugee arm of the United Nations. Their task is enormous and complicated: "the UNHCR must persuade State Parties that they must fulfill their obligations under international refugee rights instruments that they entered willingly into, presumably, in 'good will' and in 'good faith.'"[33]

Added to this is what every country in the world knows but no one seems able to fix: that the guidelines established by the 1951 Refugee Convention and the 1967 Protocol are obsolete, outdated, and causing more harm than good. But like the continual debates about the need for term limits in the United States Congress—whose members would have to do the amending of the Constitution or give state conventions that power—why would international states or countries amend or expand the criteria to be designated a refugee if it would increase their global responsibilities to take care of more refugees? A 2013 analysis of the UNHCR's struggle to supervise member states argued that a more immediate challenge is "how to protect what States have already agreed to under international refugee rights instruments, given the efforts on the part of some States to retrench the rights that refugees are entitled to presently, as opposed to trying to enhance these refugee rights."[34]

The 1951 Refugee Convention also established the principle of **nonrefoulement** (sometimes spelled non-refoulement), French for the right of nonreturn. In essence, this legal precept states that countries that are signatories to the Convention cannot return someone seeking political asylum to the country they are escaping from because it would be a denial of their human rights. However, as Lillian Robb has pointed out, countries can technically move around nonrefoulement if they feel that the migrant/asylee is a risk to the security or sovereignty of the nation.[35]

This has been especially true in Australia where migrants seeking protection can be denied that "right" if they are deemed to be in "bad character." Australia does set a high standard to determine if an asylee is not a threat: "The decision-maker must consider the seriousness of the danger posed, the likelihood of the danger being realized, the imminence of the danger, and the nature and seriousness of the risk of refoulement."[36] However, as Robb notes, Australia has a different standard compared to the Refugee Convention, which allows the government to participate in international refugee law while also subjectively applying the standard of nonrefoulement. Accordingly, "a migrant may be ineligible for the grant of a protection visa while being owed non-refoulement obligations due to the disparity between the definitions of 'particularly serious crime' and 'danger to the Australian community' in the domestic and international legislation."[37]

32. James C. Simeon,. 2013. "Introduction: Searching for Ways to Enhance the UNHCR's Capacity to Supervise International Refugee Law." In UNHCR and the Supervision of International Refugee Law. Croydon, UK: Cambridge University Press, 1–36, p. 5.

33. Ibid, p. 7.

34. Ibid, p. 8.

35. Lillian Robb. 2020. "From Cancellation to Removal: The Protection of Migrants of 'Bad Character' in Australia." American University International Law Review, 35 (2): 249–295.

36. Ibid, p. 273.

37. Ibid, p. 283.

Figure 2.4   Australian campaign to deter asylees.

List of Key Takeaways

Review the list of bullet points below for a quick overview of the key ideas and information in this chapter:

- It is unfair and historically inaccurate to not examine the Holocaust when learning about refugee policy and law.
- This is especially important because there are still people who deny the Holocaust ever occurred, which causes further trauma for the victims and their descendants.
- Although World War II technically began in September 1939, attacks on Jewish people, businesses, and religious life in Germany systematically began in 1933.
- There were attempts to help refugees displaced within and outside Europe after the war, but these were often short-sighted due to a lack of consensus on who qualified for a refugee and which countries were responsible for helping.
- The 1951 Refugee Convention and 1967 Protocol created the standard definition of a refugee that is still in use today. It includes the criteria of people who feel persecuted due to their religion, race, nationality, as well as political opinions who are fearful of returning to the country of their birth.
- The Convention also established the concept of nonrefoulement, which simply means that countries cannot send or return people back to the countries and places they are trying to escape.
- Refugee law is plagued by several challenges in the twenty-first century, including a lack of international compliance and an out-of-date definition of who classifies as a refugee.

Chapter Review Questions

1. **Define** the *Kristallnacht*, and explain its effect on Jewish people.
2. **Interpret** this statement in the context of the plight of refugees fleeing Europe: "The Great Depression also hung over the United States like a funereal fog."
3. **Which** of the following criteria for persecution is *not* included in the U.N.'s original refugee definition?
    a. Race
    b. **Sexuality (CORRECT)**
    c. Religion
    d. Nationality
4. **Identify** TWO international refugee organizations created before the 1951 Refugee Convention.
5. **Explain** why Australia might be violating the principle of nonrefoulement.
6. **Name** ONE reason compliance is a particular challenge with international refugee law.

Critical Thinking Prompts

1. **Develop** an argument related to sovereignty that supports Lebanon's decision to NOT ratify the 1951 Refugee Convention.
2. **Recommend** THREE ways for students to draw parallels or lessons between the Holocaust and Syrian Refugee Crisis.
3. **Hypothesize** a theory to explain why it is still difficult, eighty years later, to blame the United States as unsupportive of Jewish refugees during World War II.
4. **Appraise** the role of Raphael Lemkin in the development of an international consensus on how refugees should be defined.

CHAPTER 3

Immigration and Naturalization

Opening Vignette

In 2015, the online magazine *Medium* started collecting immigrants' stories to document the inexplicable realities and challenges of becoming a U.S. citizen, receiving political asylum, avoiding deportation, and just trying to figure out how the system works. One story illustrates that even serving in the military may not be enough to naturalize. After serving in the Ecuadorian Army, Fernando Sacoto decided to move to the United States without applying for a visa. After an intense journey through four countries, he reached the U.S. with the help of smugglers by hiding in the trunk of a car. He made his way from California to New Jersey and decided that he wanted to stay in his new home at all costs. After being swindled by some so-called lawyers, Sacoto enlisted in the U.S. Army.

Accordingly, "A few weeks into basic training, I learned that my latest attempt to legalize my status was fraudulent. Since I was in the Army already, I stayed quiet. I was very proud to serve in the best army of the world, ready to defend the country that gave me the opportunity to have a better life." Sacoto served with distinction and after leaving the Army, worked a number of jobs and eventually started his own business. In 2003, after 17 years of living undocumented in the United States, he became a U.S. citizen through a process set up to naturalize veterans and active-duty military. He wrote, "The truth is that I considered myself an American the day I enlisted in the Army and was willing to make the ultimate sacrifice for this country."[1]

But not every immigrant-turned-veteran's story is one of redemption. Tijuana, Mexico, is the base of an unusual and heartbreaking organization: Unified United States Deported Veterans (UUSDV),[2] who assist American veterans who have been deported to Mexico and struggle to adjust to life in a country many never really knew. UUSDV maintains a network of deported veterans and helps with family reunification, job training, etc. Repatriate Our Patriots, a similar organization, contends that the Biden administration has made some efforts on the issue but not enough. Deported veterans must first apply for humanitarian parolee status—ironically, the same process and designation for the recent evacuees from Afghanistan (which we discussed in Chapter 1)—but that does not guarantee they will be allowed back in the U.S. and finally be naturalized as citizens.[3]

---

1. Fernando Sacoto. 2015. "How I Earned My Citizenship Defending This Country." My Time in Line: What it Really Takes for U.S. Immigrants to Get Legal Status (Medium), November 18. https://medium.com/@fernandosacoto/how-i-earned-my-citizenship-defending-this-country-5fdfd76aac

2. https://www.uusdepvets.org/

3. Kristian Hernández. 2023. "White House Initiative Leaves Deported Veterans in Limbo." The Center for Public Integrity (Immigration). https://publicintegrity.org/inequality-poverty-opportunity/immigration/white-house-initiative-leaves-deported-veterans-in-limbo/

Introduction to the Chapter

The fundamental difference between immigrants and refugees is one of situation and intent; immigration is voluntary and often with a specific destination and new home in mind, but "refugees are forced to migrate."[4] Nothing in the United States, however, is this simple, and as the opening stories illustrate, there are many paths to enter the United States and *pathways* to citizenship. This has become abundantly clear with the recent wave of migrants into the United States, since 2023, who are not refugees (because many are seeking asylum, but their applications have not been approved or will likely not be approved[5]) and also not immigrants because most do not have legal authorization to enter the U.S. on an immigrant visa. This has resulted in tension and even violence between these newer migrants and existing immigrant communities.[6] Further, not everyone who comes to the United States intends on staying permanently. And why are all refugees immigrants, but not all immigrants are refugees? According to one sociologist,

> While present-day U.S. legislation clearly differentiates between refugees (who left their native countries because of persecution or fears of persecution) and immigrants (who come to the U.S. to be reunited with family members or for economic reasons), social scientists disagree on how important the refugee-immigrant distinction is.[7]

This chapter will broaden your understanding of immigration to the United States and place it in historical context. Refugees are one type of immigrant with a very specific and special need, but there are almost 200 types of visas issued by the federal government that cover immigrants (who want to stay in the U.S.) and nonimmigrants. While refugees fall in the first group, the story of United States immigration politics and policy is much bigger. We will demystify the study of immigration and provide historical context as to how the United States has viewed immigration from the eighteenth century to the present; the rise of nativists and anti-immigrant voices; and what the human nature of immigration looks like with data and statistics.

4. Shyam K. Sriram. 2018. "The Politics of Refugee Resettlement." PhD Dissertation, University of California at Santa Barbara, p. 4.

5. Hurubie Meko, and Raúl Vilchis. 2023. "New Migrants Have a Year to Apply for Asylum. Many Won't Make It." *The New York Times*, July 3. https://www.nytimes.com/2023/07/03/nyregion/migrants-asylum-nyc.html.

6. Rafael Bernal. 2023. "Tensions Rise between New and Established Migrants." The Hill, October 29. https://thehill.com/latino/4279680-tensions-new-established-migrants/.

7. Bernadette Ludwig. 2016. "The Different Meanings of the Word Refugee." In Refugee Resettlement in the United States: Language, Policy, Pedagogy, eds. Emily M. Feuerherm and Vaidehi Ramanathan. Bristol, UK: Multilingual Matters, p. 37.

Looking at the Data

- In the 2022 fiscal year, the United States issued 6,815,120 nonimmigrant visas.[8]
- Almost half of the nonimmigrant visas (3,228,199) went to people visiting for "business and pleasure."[9]
- However, only 493,448 immigrant visas were issued in the same year.[10]
- Between July 1 and September 30, 2022 (third quarter or Q3), "280,000 noncitizens obtained lawful permanent resident (LPR) status."[11]
- 38% of these new LPRs were from just five countries: the Philippines, India, Mexico, China, and the Dominican Republic.[12]

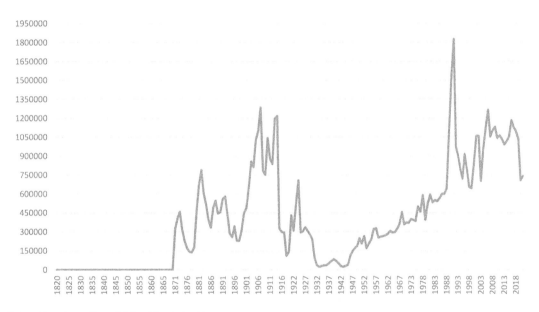

Figure 3.1   New Legal/Lawful Residents by Year.

Data Source: https://www.dhs.gov/sites/default/files/2023-03/2022_1114_plcy_yearbook_immigration_statistics_fy2021_v2_1.pdf.

8. Bureau of Consular Affairs. 2022. "Table XV (A): Classes of Nonimmigrant Visas (Including Border Crossing Cards) Fiscal Years 2018–2022." Nonimmigrant Visa Statistics (Multi-Year Reports), U.S. Department of State. https://travel.state.gov/content/dam/visas/Statistics/AnnualReports/FY2022AnnualReport/FY22_TableXV(A).pdf

9. Ibid.

10. US Department of State. 2022. "Table III: Immigrant Visas Issued (by Foreign State of Chargeability or Place of Birth) Fiscal Year 2022." Summary of Visas Issued by Issuing Office: Fiscal Year 2022 (Report of the Visa Office 2022). https://travel.state.gov/content/dam/visas/Statistics/AnnualReports/FY2022AnnualReport/FY22_TableIII.pdf

11. US Department of Homeland Security. 2022. "Recent Trends." Legal Immigration and Adjustment of Status Report Fiscal Year 2022, Quarter 3. https://www.dhs.gov/immigration-statistics/special-reports/legal-immigration

12. Ibid, "Countries of Nationality."

Learning Objectives

Reading this chapter will enable readers to:

- **Differentiate** between patriotism, nationalism, and nativism.
- **Describe** early efforts at the "Americanization" of immigrants.
- **Interpret** immigration statistics, and **discuss** the challenges to naturalization.

Immigration and Nativism

From the mid-eighteenth century to the late nineteenth century, the federal government had almost no role to play with immigration restriction.[13] The new states, previously colonies, handled their own needs and obtained their own workers who often came from overseas (especially the system of slavery and forced labor that was normalized in the Southeast through the nineteenth century). Even at this time, immigrants were not treated equally. According to Robert Bellah, "All Americans except the Indians are immigrants or the descendents [sic] of immigrants, but not all immigrants have met the same reception."[14]

Acclaimed historian Ronald Takaki has argued that two of the most influential people in early American history regarding immigration were Benjamin Rush and Thomas Jefferson. The former, also known as the Father of American Medicine, believed in racial purity and had severely negative views about immigration. Jefferson, according to Takaki, supported "republican machines"—that would teach new immigrants the key values to be ideal citizens. Both men were in favor of education but only if it benefited immigrants who could reach the same societal status as white people.[15] Another early supporter of what would later be called "Americanization" was Benjamin Franklin, who disliked non-Anglo Saxon immigrants.[16]

A prominent sociologist once wrote how "Americans have always passed rules encouraging the arrival of some people while discouraging the arrival of others."[17] This has been true from the very beginning, including language on naturalization (i.e., who could become a citizen) outlined in Article 1, Section 8 of the Constitution: "[The Congress shall have Power …] To establish an uniform Rule of Naturalization, and uniform Laws on the subject of Bankruptcies throughout the United States."[18] This was followed by the Naturalization Act of 1790, which limited citizenship only to a "free white person," clarified policy on the children of citizens, and which institution should oversee naturalization (the judiciary).[19] This is the beginning of the intrinsic American association between race and

---

13. Philip G. Schrag. 2000. A Well-Founded Fear: The Congressional Battle to Save Political Asylum in America. New York: Routledge, p. 18.

14. Robert N. Bellah. 1989 (1975). The Broken Covenant: American Civil Religion in Time of Trial. Chicago: The University of Chicago Press, p. 88.

15. Ronald Takaki. 2000 (1979). Iron Cages: Race and Culture in 19th-Century America. New York: Oxford University Press.

16. Bellah. (1989).

17. John S. W. Park. 2018. Immigration Law and Society. Medford, MA: Polity Press, p. 26.

18. Congressional Research Service. 2022. "Art1.S8.C4.1.2.3. Early U.S. Naturalization Laws." Constitution of the United States: Analysis and Interpretation. https://constitution.congress.gov/browse/essay/artI-S8-C4-1-2-3/ALDE_00013163/

19. Ibid.

citizenship.[20] Congress followed the 1790 Naturalization Act with the even more specific 1798 Alien And Sedition Acts, which explicitly restricted the political rights, if any, of naturalized Americans. Now seen as explicitly partisan and a Federalist Party weapon to eviscerate the Democratic-Republican Party, the acts "increased the residency requirement for American citizenship from five to fourteen years, authorized the president to imprison or deport aliens considered "dangerous to the peace and safety of the United States" and restricted speech critical of the government."[21]

One of the most misunderstood political ideologies is nativism. It would be insufficient to describe a nativist as someone opposed to immigration because *some* immigration is seen by nativists as a good thing. Nativists believe that immigration is good if it benefits the country by contribution to a sense of shared nationalism and pride based on similar ethnic, racial, and linguistic traits. As recently as December 2023, former President Donald Trump expressed nativist sentiment at a rally: "They let—I think the real number is 15, 16 million people into our country. When they do that, we got a lot of work to do. They're poisoning the blood of our country … They poison mental institutions and prisons all over the world."[22] Nativists call themselves patriots, but they are not, because they do not believe everyone in the United States, even citizens, should have the same rights or are good for the country. Robert Welch, who founded the John Birch Society, was a key nativist in American history. "His Americanism," a biographer writes,

> cast suspicion on so-called hyphenism, whether German American, African American, or Italian American. In wartime America, many German Americans faced an onslaught against their ethnic institutions and language and were pressured to Americanize. Welch cheered that development … Nativism became confused with patriotism. It was America first.[23]

To put it another way, nativism in the United States is the belief that only European immigrants who identify as white (or perceived as such) and were mostly Protestant could contribute positively to the growth and future of the United States. A classic understanding of nativism comes from the work of John Higham who coined this definition in 1955:

> Whether the nativist was a workingman or a Protestant evangelist, a southern conservative or a northern reformer, he stood for a certain kind of nationalism. He believed … that some influence originating abroad threatened the very life of the nation from within … nativism translates them into a zeal to destroy the enemies of a distinctively American way of life.[24]

20. Takaki. (2000).

21. Ken Drexler. 2019. "Alien and Sedition Acts: Primary Documents in American History." Library of Congress (Research Guides), September 27. https://guides.loc.gov/alien-and-sedition-acts

22. Ginger Gibson. 2023. "Trump Says Immigrants Are 'Poisoning the Blood of Our Country.' Biden Campaign Likens Comments to Hitler." NBC News, December 17. https://www.nbcnews.com/politics/2024-election/trump-says-immigrants-are-poisoning-blood-country-biden-campaign-liken-rcna130141

23. Edward H. Miller. 2022. A Conspiratorial Life: Robert Welch, the John Birch Society, and the Revolution of American Conservatism. Chicago: University of Chicago Press, p. 46.

24. John Higham. 1988 (1955). Strangers in the Land: Patterns of American Nativism, 1860–1925. New Brunswick, NJ: Rutgers University Press, p. 4.

A more recent understanding is that nativism is "opposition to immigration that is based on fears that the immigrating group will erode or change existing cultural values … Nativistic movements also emerge when immigrants outnumber original inhabitants."[25] The irony in all of this is that the phrase is not in reference to Native Americans and the indigenous people, who were displaced by the colonists; rather, "the inhabitants of the first 13 British colonies who sought to cultivate particular cultural values."[26]

What many young people fail to recognize is how deep the roots go with anti-Catholic attitudes in the United States. These opinions developed in Europe and were literally exported to the United States with the early colonists, who especially targeted Irish Catholic immigrants as early as 1820![27] If it started with the Irish, American nativism really took off in response to other European immigrants, who were not seen as white or Protestant enough; later, the Chinese would be added to the list of nativists' enemies. As Figure 3.1 shows, American immigration exploded around the Civil War with the number of new lawful residents spiking and falling for a few decades before a steady incline in the mid-twentieth century.

Chinese laborers suffered inhumane levels of discrimination and violence, including mob "justice" like lynchings. "In the era of Chinese exclusion," wrote one political scientist, "being American meant not being Chinese."[28] Nativist anger, just like the earlier 1790 Naturalization Act and 1798 Alien and Sedition Acts, spilled over into Congress with the passage of the 1882 Chinese Exclusion Act. Some of the legislation included:

- "… until the expiration of ten years next after the passage of this act, the coming of Chinese laborers to the United States be … suspended."
- "That no Chinese person shall be permitted to enter the United States by land without producing to the proper officer of customs the certificate in this act required of Chinese persons seeking to land from a vessel. And any Chinese person found unlawfully within the United States shall be caused to be removed therefrom to the country from whence he came, by direction of the President of the United States."
- "That hereafter no State court or court of the United States shall admit Chinese to citizenship; and all laws in conflict with this act are hereby repealed."[29]

The Question: Was it legal for the United States to deny citizenship to Chinese immigrants and their families just fourteen years after amending the Constitution to guarantee birthright citizenship in 1868?

25. Jill Y. Crainshaw. 2013. "Nativism." In Encyclopedia of Religious Controversies in the United States, 2nd Edition, p. 541–542.
26. Ibid, p. 542.
27. Ray Billington. 1938. The Protestant Crusade, 1800 to 1860: A Study of the Origins of American Nativism. New York: Macmillan.
28. Tom K. Wong. 2017. The Politics of Immigration: Partisanship, Democratic Change, and American National Identity. New York: Oxford University Press, p. 2.
29. National Archives. 2023. "Chinese Exclusion Act (1882)." The U.S. National Archives and Records Administration (Milestone Documents). https://www.archives.gov/milestone-documents/chinese-exclusion-act

The Americanization Movement

A lot of Americans use the phrase "progressive" now to describe candidates or policy positions that are seen as more forward thinking than what other people believe. Too few people, unfortunately, are not aware of the Progressive Era in the early twentieth century. Those Progressives were seen as social reformers who wanted to find the root causes of a lot of social problems in America. These men and women are celebrated for their foresight, but most Americans do not know that the Progressives blamed a specific group for causing most of the problems in the United States: immigrants. Part of the reason, according to political scientist James Morone, is that our society's call to liberty has made the U.S. "susceptible to moral combustions"—who is *more* American and more entitled to tell others what to feel and believe. This becomes a "vaguely delineated, highly moralistic code of conduct. Flunk and you're un-American. A society on full boil keeps stirring up the same deep tribal fears: These others do not share our values. They do not understand our religious traditions. They will subvert the virtues that made us rise and prosper."[30]

One such Progressive was Frances Kellor, who insisted the national government needed to be more involved in not only immigration, but who could become American. She was regarded as one of the first experts on immigration and a close advisor to President Theodore Roosevelt.[31] Congress was also swayed by Kellor and in 1906, created the U.S. Bureau of Naturalization.[32]

The Progressives were so influential that Roosevelt authorized Congress to fund a national panel to study immigration. The Dillingham Commission met from 1907 to 1911 and focused much of its work on lifting Americans out of poverty, which it saw as the straight path toward Americanization.[33] Immigrants, who, at this time, often constituted a majority of the poor, became the target to "fix" poverty. Like Thomas Jefferson and Benjamin Rush, educating the poor became the mantra of the Progressives and was also seen as the vehicle to make people more American.[34] In the short term, the Dillingham Commission suggested several proposals, most of which never became law or were never implemented. But there is an argument that the Commission's work formed the foundation of anti-Communist sentiment during the Red Scare when "those who did not fit traditional white, Anglo-Saxon American norms became the targets of mistrust, suspected malefactors whose potential for disruption had to be checked."[35]

Like earlier pieces of legislation, the United States Congress would continue to restrict immigration through the 1921 Quota Law, 1924 Immigration Act Origins Law, and 1952 Immigration and Nationality Act. This was done

30. Ibid.

31. Theodore Roosevelt Center. "Frances Kellor." TR Encyclopedia (Dickinson State University). https://www.theodorerooseveltcenter.org/Learn-About-TR/TR-Encyclopedia/Politics-and-Government/Frances-Kellor.aspx

32. Higham (1988, 241).

33. Robert F. Zeidel. 2004. Immigrants, Progressives, and Exclusion Politics: The Dillingham Commission, 1900–1927. DeKalb, IL: Northern Illinois University Press.

34. Irene Bloemraad, and Reed Ueda. 2006. "Naturalization and Nationality." In a Companion to American Immigration, ed. Reed Ueda. Malden, MA: Blackwell Publishing, p. 41.

35. Zeidel. (2004, 145).

in three steps: "first by refusing to facilitate immigration, then by imposing qualitative restrictions on immigrants, and finally by limiting the number as well as the kind of immigrants accepted each year."[36]

Federal and state courts were also very active during this era, trying to codify who qualified as white, an early condition of citizenship. There were at least 52 cases decided between 1878 and 1944 that covered the Chinese (*In re Ah Up* [1878]); (*In re Kanaka Nian* [1889]); Burmese (*In re Po* [1894]); Japanese (*In re Saito* [1894]), *Bessho v. U.S.* (1910), *Ozawa v. U.S.* (1922); Koreans (*Petition of EasurkEmsen Charr* [1921]); Afghanis (*In re Feroz Din* [1928]); Arabs (*In re Ahmed Hassan* [1942]), *Ex parteMohriez* (1944); and Filipinos in five cases between 1916 and 1941. In some cases, Asian Indians and Syrians were not white and later white.[37]

However, it was World War I and the almost overnight threat of Germany—people, language, values—in the United States that accelerated efforts to "Americanize" immigrants. This era also created the dichotomy of the good versus bad immigrant; good immigrants spoke English and the postwar goal was "100-percent Americanism."[38] The pro-English, anti-every-other-language surge was so zealous that President Roosevelt allegedly said, "Hereafter we must see that the melting pot really does not melt. There should be but one language in this country—the English."[39] One of the most infamous examples of the thinking of that era was Henry Ford's English School for his workers. At the graduation ceremony, "A giant pot was built outside the gates of his factory into which danced groups of gaily dressed immigrants singing their native songs. From the other side of the pot emerged a single stream of Americans clad in the contemporary standard dress and singing the national anthem."[40]

Passed during World War I and over President Woodrow Wilson's veto, the Immigration Act of 1917 was the first piece of legislation to emphasize a literacy test for naturalization, a form of which still continues to the current day in the citizenship test administered by the United States Citizenship and Immigration Services (USCIS). Interestingly enough, one group of applicants was exempt from an English test: those who had faced "religious persecution" before emigrating.[41] However, the 1917 Immigration Act still provided plenty of institutional discrimination; it created an "Asiatic barred zone" and an $8 immigrant tax. This would be just over $200 in 2023![42] Additionally, the law "restricted the immigration of people with mental and physical disabilities, the poor, and people with criminal records or suspected of being involved in prostitution."[43]

36. Philip L. Martin, Philip L. and Marion F. Houston. 1984. "European and American Immigration Policies." In U.S. Immigration Policy, ed. Richard R. Hofstetter. Durham, NC: Duke University Press, p. 30.

37. Wong. (2017, 26).

38. Higham. (1993, 53).

39. Hiroshi Motomura. 2006. Americans in Waiting: The Lost Story of Immigration and Citizenship in America. New York: Oxford University Press, p. 170.

40. Bellah. (1989, 94).

41. Doug Coulson. 2017. Race, Nation, and Refuge: The Rhetoric of Race in Asian American Citizenship Cases. Albany, NY: SUNY Press, p. 86.

42. https://www.dollartimes.com/inflation/inflation.php?amount=8&year=1917

43. Equal Justice Initiative. "Immigration Act of 1917 Bans Asians, Other Non-White People from Entering U.S." On this Day—Feb 05, 1917. https://calendar.eji.org/racial-injustice/feb/05

From the Collections of The Henry Ford

Figure 3.2   Graduation ceremony at the Ford English School, July 4, 1917.

Ford Motor Company, https://www.thehenryford.org/collections-and-research/digital-collections/artifact/254569, 1917.

A Visa for Everything

In this section, we pivot to some of the most important pieces of legislation of the twentieth century and then look at the current state of immigration. Several historic events collided in the reshaping of American immigration policy in the middle of the twentieth century, including post-World War II prosperity, the Baby Boom generation, the need for technical expertise during the Cold War, etc. As we discussed in Chapters 1 and 2, the Holocaust and the displacement of those who survived the Nazi horrors demanded an urgent and global need to resettle and move people from harm to safety. The 1951 Refugee Convention may have created a global standard, but individual countries also passed their own laws in response. One of these was the 1952 Immigration and Nationality Act, which clarified policy on naturalization, terrorism, alien removal, and immigration, broadly.[44] It also codified the American position on refugees (though that would not really be fleshed out until the 1980 Refugee Act as we talked about earlier in this textbook) and upheld national quotas that favored immigration from Western countries but not much from Asia, the Middle East, and Africa. Like the 1917 Immigration Act, it was also not supported by the president—this

44. US Citizenship and Immigration Services. 2019. "Immigration and Nationality Act." U.S. Department of Homeland Security. https://www.uscis.gov/laws-and-policy/legislation/immigration-and-nationality-act

time Harry Truman—and was passed into law through a congressional veto.[45] One of the more controversial aspects related to its co-sponsor, Senator Pat McCarran (D-Nevada), who said about the bill,

> … we have in the United States today hard-core, indigestible blocs which have not become integrated into the American way of life, but which, on the contrary are its deadly enemies. Today, as never before, untold millions are storming our gates for admission, and those gates are cracking under the strain.[46]

This law would not last for too long; less than fifteen years later, it would be abrogated by new policy, championed by a president whose death would shatter the country but whose legislative wishes would become policy soon thereafter. To call the 1965 Immigration and Nationality Act a landmark law would be an understatement. It fundamentally reversed two centuries of nativist and institutionally—and structurally—racist immigration policy, allowing millions of people to emigrate to the United States who had been denied for too long (including this author's parents who arrived just as the Vietnam War concluded).

The Immigration and Naturalization Act of 1965

- Known as the Hart-Celler Act to honor Rep. Emanuel Celler and Senator Philip Hart.
- The bill was first introduced by President John F. Kennedy in 1963 but signed into law by Kennedy's successor, President Lyndon B. Johnson, in 1965 after Kennedy was assassinated.[47]
- Before 1965, the United States had a system of "national-origins quotas … [which] created a preference for immigration from countries in Northwestern Europe, loosely restricted immigration from Southern and Eastern Europe, and tightly restricted immigration from Asia, Africa, and the colonized Caribbean."[48]
- The INA substituted quotas for "per-country ceilings" and created whole categories of immigration for spouses, relatives, siblings, family members, professionals, those with advanced degrees, and skilled workers.[49]

---

45. Marion T. Bennett. 1966. "The Immigration and Nationality (McCarran-Walter) Act of 1952, as Amended to 1965." The Annals of the American Academy of Political and Social Science 367: 127–36.

46. Kevin J. Baker. 2016. "Living in LBJ's America." The New York Times (Opinion), August 28. https://www.nytimes.com/2016/08/28/opinion/campaign-stops/living-in-lbjs-america.html

47. Jerry Kammer. 2015. "The Hart-Celler Immigration Act of 1965." Center for Immigration Studies, September 30. https://cis.org/Report/HartCeller-Immigration-Act-1965

48. David S. FitzGerald, and David Cook-Martin. 2015. "The Geopolitical Origins of the U.S. Immigration Act of 1965." The Online Journal of the Migration Policy Institute, February 5. https://www.migrationpolicy.org/article/geopolitical-origins-us-immigration-act-1965

49. Ballotpedia. "Immigration and Naturalization Act of 1965." https://ballotpedia.org/Immigration_and_Naturalization_Act_of_1965

According to federal data, the number of naturalization petitions has steadily increased since the government started keeping track. In 1907, there were 21,113 petitions filed and only 7,941 approvals (just under 38%). By 1943, approvals had skyrocketed to 84.5%, undoubtedly affected by the emergency of World War II and displacement. Petitions dropped considerably in the postwar years but quickly rebounded through the 1950s and 1960s, partly due to a new class of immigrants fleeing Communism (as we discussed in Chapter 1). The 1990s proved to be a defining decade for immigration during the Clinton administration; in 1996 alone, the federal government approved 1,040,991 of 1,277,403 naturalization petitions, or 81.4%.

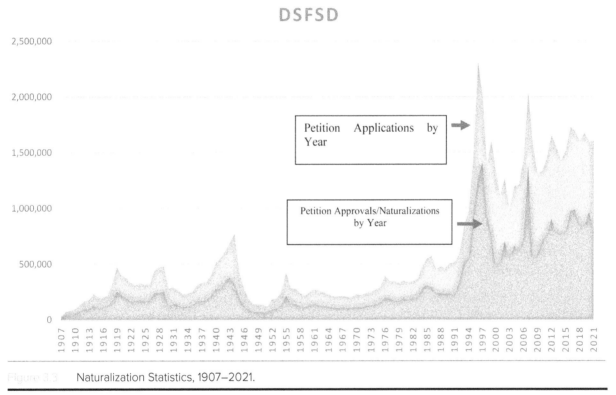

Figure 3.3   Naturalization Statistics, 1907–2021.

Data Source: https://www.dhs.gov/immigration-statistics/naturalizations

There are just under 30 different visas for nonimmigrants, including special visas for everything from airline and ship crew members (D-Class) and athletes, entertainers, and artists (P-Class) to fiancé(e)s (K-Class) and religious representatives (R-Class). One visa type that might be of interest to you is the student visa (F-Class). If someone wants to study at a college, university, language training program, high school, or even a seminary, they will need a student visa; this is an important point, which also means that a nonimmigrant visitor on a tourist visa cannot attend college in the United States.[50]

50. Bureau of Consular Affairs. "Student Visa." U.S. Department of State. https://travel.state.gov/content/travel/en/us-visas/study/student-visa.html

Table 3. 1: Student vs. Total Nonimmigrant Visas per Year, 2018 to 2022[51]

	Student Visas	Total
2018	389,579	9,028,026
2019	388,839	8,742,068
2020	121,205	4,013,210
2021	377,659	2,792,083
2022	437,018	6,815,120

List of Key Takeaways

Review the list of bullet points below for a quick overview of the key ideas and information in this chapter:

- Refugees are a type of immigrants who come to the United States, but unlike most other immigrants, did not voluntarily leave and often cannot return to their country of origin.
- Most of the early congressional legislation on immigration was related to naturalization, who could become a citizen, and the political rights of noncitizens.
- Nativism was an American political ideology that developed in the nineteenth century and is still felt today. The earliest nativist movement targeted Catholics.
- Nativists believe that only some immigration and immigrants are good for America, and it is often but not always tied to race and religion. Anyone who is not seen as a good immigrant is consequentially bad for the United States.
- European and Asian emigration in the nineteenth and twentieth centuries was met with resistance by many who started to push for more "Americanization" to make English and civics classes mandatory and to make it more difficult for people to become citizens.
- These efforts would lead to the eventual creation of a citizenship test still used today.
- The United States fundamentally changed its stance on immigration in 1965 when the Immigration and Nationality Act removed country-specific quotas.
- The two broad visa categories in the United States are immigrant (plan on living here full time) versus nonimmigrant (visiting for work and school).

51. Bureau of Consular Affairs. 2022. "Table XV (A): Classes of Nonimmigrant Visas (Including Border Crossing Cards) Fiscal Years 2018-2022." Nonimmigrant Visa Statistics (Multi-Year Reports), U.S. Department of State. https://travel.state.gov/content/dam/visas/Statistics/AnnualReports/FY2022AnnualReport/FY22_TableXV(A).pdf.

Chapter Review Questions

1. **Name** one difference between immigrants and refugees.
2. **What** are the two broad categories of visas?
3. **Identify** the key demographic eligible for citizenship in the Naturalization Act of 1790.
   a. Free white veterans
   b. White Anglo-Saxon Protestants
   c. **Free white person (CORRECT)**
   d. White men and women
4. **What** was one result of the 1921 Quota Law, 1924 Immigration Act Origins Law, and 1952 Immigration and Nationality Act?
   a. Immigration increased to record levels
   b. All immigration was halted until 1965
   c. **Immigration restrictions continued for certain groups of people (CORRECT)**
   d. President Trump would later use all three as justification for building a wall
5. **Why** did President Theodore Roosevelt say, "the melting pot really does not melt"?
6. **Recall** the name of the federal agency that approves all citizenship applications.
   a. United States Customs and Border Patrol (CBP)
   b. Department of Homeland Security (DHS)
   c. **United States Citizenship and Immigration Services (USCIS) (CORRECT)**
   d. Bureau of Population, Refugees, and Migration (BPRM)

Critical Thinking Prompts

1. **Compare** the veterans' stories at the beginning of the chapter. How do these testimonies affirm or constrict our understanding of veterans and patriotism?
2. Professor John S. W. Park famously wrote, "Americans have always passed rules encouraging the arrival of some people while discouraging the arrival of others." Drawing on Park, **build** your own definition of nativism that includes a recent example.
3. **Elaborate** on the idea of an "intrinsic American association between race and citizenship."
4. **How** did President Kennedy's death shape immigration policy?
5. **Why** is it problematic to use the term "progressive" so loosely in the United States now?

CHAPTER 4

A Comparative Look at Immigration

Opening Vignette

One of the most fascinating refugee communities in the United States are the Hmong (pronounced Mung), a stateless nationality that owes their origins to Southeast Asia and are most often associated with Laos and Cambodia but are often neither Laotian nor Cambodian by ethnicity. Many Hmong also fought and died in the Secret War, a CIA-backed military operation in Laos through the 1960s and 1970s.[1] The Hmong are also unique due to their religious practices, which combine animism with "a distinctive system of household-based rituals that affirm their connection to ancestors and kin and facilitated spiritual well-being."[2]

Figure 4.1   Hmong Story Cloth depicting birth of Jesus with Hmong village life.

Houa Yang/Catawba County Library, https://commons.wikimedia.org/wiki/File:Folk_Tale_Story_Cloth_-_DPLA_-_311731f49d29f218c4658671f175b8f7.jpg.

1. Pa Nhia Xiong. 2020. "The Secret War: The Forgotten Hmong Heroes." PhD Dissertation, California State University, Fresno. https://scholarworks.calstate.edu/downloads/3r074x44x
2. Melissa May Borja. 2023. Follow the New Way: American Refugee Resettlement Policy and Hmong Religious Change. Cambridge, MA: Harvard University Press, p. 4.

Hmong refugees started to resettle in the United States in the 1970s, and the following decades identified with this traditional religious practice. But that is not the situation now. Most Hmong Americans now identify as Christian, and there are hundreds of Hmong churches in every possible Christian denomination across the country. This is not just a story about religious conversion. According to Dr. Melissa Borja, Christianity became the favored religion among Hmong Americans because it "allowed them to acquire new ways of managing old spiritual problems."[3] Borja points out that many Hmong practice Christianity in combination with their traditional beliefs as a form of "lived religion." She also acknowledges that Hmong refugees carried so much trauma with them through the violence and horror of war and displacement that they relied heavily on volunteers, agencies, and other assistance, most of it Christian-based and oriented.[4]

Figure 4.2   2022 Resettlement Affiliates.

Bureau of Population, Refugees, and Migration, https://www.wrapsnet.org/documents/2614-PRM-FY22-Affiliate-Sites-8.5x11.pdf, U.S Department of State 2022.

CWS: Church World Service
ECDC: Ethiopian Community Development Council
EMM: Episcopal Migration Ministries
HIAS

IRC: International Rescue Committee
LIRS: Lutheran Immigration and Refugee Service
USCCB: United States Conference of Catholic Bishops

USCRI: U.S. Committee for Refugees and Immigrants
WR: World Relief
○ Multiple sites

There are no affiliate sites in American Samoa, Guam, or Puerto Rico.

Figure 4.3   Map Key.

Bureau of Population, Refugees, and Migration, https://www.wrapsnet.org/documents/2614-PRM-FY22-Affiliate-Sites-8.5x11.pdf, U.S Department of State 2022.

3. Ibid, p. 7.
4. Ibid, p. 11.

As the affiliates map shows us, the only two nonreligious organizations resettling refugees in the United States are the International Rescue Committee and the Committee for Refugees and Immigrants. All the others are various Christian denominations and Jewish (HIAS stands for Hebrew Immigrant Aid Society).

Introduction to the Chapter

This is something that truly separates resettlement policy in the United States from that of other countries: a public-private partnership between federal institutions—the president, Congress, federal agencies—with private, often religious-based organizations to resettle refugees across the country while also working with state and local governments. No other country in the world relies so much in the twenty-first century on religious-based individuals and nonprofit organizations to carry out resettlement. One reason is less acceptance globally of association between Christian-based organizations and what is sometimes termed "white saviorism." Those doubts about separating religion from social services have also manifested in recent scrutiny and public apologies over the treatment of Native American and indigenous children in the United States and Canada in government-funded, Christian-run residential schools.

One apparent contradiction of the United States's resettlement program is the reliance on private actors who are most often affiliated with Christian churches and agencies. The notion of a "contradiction" primarily comes from the realization that refugee resettlement is often viewed as a secular (nonreligious) government policy. However, as Borja has mentioned,

> We wouldn't have a refugee resettlement program if we didn't have private voluntary agencies doing the work in collaboration with the government. And in particular, we wouldn't have those private voluntary agencies doing this work if it weren't for religious institutions.[5]

The role of religious groups in refugee resettlement is an arrangement not without controversy, but it does not seem likely to change anytime soon. There is a long history of Christian-based organizations involved in every aspect of welfare and social services in the United States from the seventeenth century to the present. We see Protestant and Catholic organizations today that cover everything from education to adoption, addiction to suicide support groups.[6] Borja asks, "When government delegates public work to private religious organizations, how does this arrangement shape people's religious beliefs, practices, and identities?"[7] While that question is not the focus of this chapter, it is part of a broader discussion of how refugee resettlement is carried out comparatively in different countries. What are the differences between assimilation and integration? How do other countries handle refugee integration, and how is it prioritized? These are some of the questions you will find answers to in this chapter.

There was a time when the United States was the world leader in accepting and resettling refugees, but we are

5. Faith and Prejudice Institute. 2022. "Religion and Refugees: The Role of Christians in Refugee Resettlement." September 24. https://youtu.be/n9GZgEoKrpE

6. It is important to note that while most Christian-based organizations offer social services to reduce poverty and improve the lives of people, there are some anti-immigration and antirefugee organizations that are grounded in Christian nationalism and hateful rhetoric.

7. Borja. 2023, 14.

not even in the top 10 anymore! This fact tends to jar Americans who love to talk about this country as the melting pot and a haven for immigration. Telling ourselves that we are "a nation of immigrants" repeatedly makes it difficult to accept some of our policies that now limit immigration (and obscure the devious erasure of Native Americans and crimes perpetrated against them).[8] We talked about the politicization of refugee resettlement in Chapter 1, but what has really changed over the last twenty years is how references to immigration, immigrants, and refugees are now used as heuristics or information shortcuts for voters. Heuristics are words or phrases that are used to simplify complex issues and problems.

When Republican candidates discuss immigration, it is intended to evoke imagery of hordes of hostile foreigners waiting at the border, usually the southern one, just waiting to be let into the United States and wreak havoc. This can often be achieved with just a few key phrases (heuristics). This is also known as "dog-whistle politics," a term coined by law professor Ian Haney López, to capture political rhetoric that do not "explicitly mention race but are ultimately used to refer to people of color and the various threats they apparently command."[9] Then, the same candidates reference "walls" to not only keep foreigners out but to create imagery that "walls" might keep the good people in.

As you will learn in the following pages, regional instability and tension around the world displaces people from their homes. Neighboring countries become sanctuaries for those fleeing oppression and persecution. Except for one or two governments, most of the leading countries in 2023 that house refugees border unstable countries. Less than 2% of all refugees find a permanent home in a country, and it is usually after years of displacement.[10]

The Global Refugee Crisis

- The top three countries of origin for refugees in 2023 were Syria, Afghanistan, and Ukraine. These countries represent 52% of all displaced people in the world.[11]
- In 2022, Europe was home to two of the largest refugee-hosting countries: Turkey and Germany.[12]
- However, Lebanon had the most refugees in terms of percentage of its population; based on 2022 statistics, almost one in every five people (19.8%) are refugees.[13]

---

8. Roxanne Dunbar-Ortiz. 2021. "Not a Nation of Immigrants." Monthly Review, September 1. https://monthlyreview.org/2021/09/01/not-a-nation-of-immigrants/

9. Sara Grossman. 2017. "Blog: Revisiting 'Dog-Whistle Politics.'" Othering & Belonging Institute (University of California, Berkeley), September 22: https://belonging.berkeley.edu/blog-revisiting-dog-whistle-politics

10. Benedicta Solf, and Katherine Rehberg. 2021. "The Resettlement Gap: A Record Number of Global Refugees, but Few Are Resettled." Migration Policy Institute (Migration Information Source), October 22, https://www.migrationpolicy.org/article/refugee-resettlement-gap

11. UNHCR. 2023. "Refugee Data Finder." https://www.unhcr.org/refugee-statistics/.

12. USA for UNHCR. 2022. "Noteworthy Facts and Statistics by Region/Country—Europe." https://www.unrefugees.org/refugee-facts/statistics/

13. Norwegian Refugee Council. 2022. "These 10 Countries Receive the Most Refugees." https://www.nrc.no/perspectives/2020/the-10-countries-that-receive-the-most-refugees/

Learning Objectives

Reading this chapter will enable readers to:

- **Distinguish** between theories of immigration and integration.
- **Inspect** the avenues available for refugees to integrate in host countries.
- **Understand** the cultural, historical, and political reasons why Chad, Germany, and Bangladesh host refugees.

The Limitations of Assimilation and the Hope of Integration

When you reach Chapter 7 and the conclusion, you will see that the pressure to integrate into American society comes with some severe consequences for refugees. But what exactly is integration? And how do different countries respond to integrating refugees and new immigrants into new ways of life? As the immigration landscape changed rapidly in the United States after the 1965 Immigration and Nationality Act (which was discussed in Chapter 3), sociologists and other scholars started to reflect on the processes and environment that changed or converted immigrants into citizens.

While becoming citizens was important—that process is known as naturalization—it was all the other new ways of thinking about what an American identity really meant that concerned people in this country. If you recall, we discussed the Americanization movement of the twentieth century in Chapter 3 and how some Americans were fearful of what immigration and new immigrants represented—a feeling that our national identity would change for the worse.

The late American sociologist Milton Gordon is credited with the Seven Stages of Assimilation, which range from cultural assimilation to civic assimilation.[14] The process of assimilation was a slow one, and over time, an individual allegedly would lose their traditional language and customs, replacing those with English and a certain American approach to life. However, Gordon himself noted that even earlier theories like Anglo-conformity and the melting pot were predicated on European immigrants and identity and left little room for others.[15] And if such room existed, it was under the assumption that European, white identity was the goal of assimilation; the idea of a melting pot where immigrants would melt completely so that immigrants would all just become one undistinguishable American mass.[16]

Scholars have also criticized Milton Gordon for not accepting that assimilation looked great on paper but less so in reality.[17] Another flaw in the theory is that the host society remains unchanged by the arrival of immigrants

14. Milton M. Gordon. 1964. Assimilation in American life: The Role of Race, Religion, and National Origins. New York: Oxford University Press.

15. Milton M. Gordon. 1961. "Assimilation in America: Theory and Reality." Daedalus, 90 (2): 263–285.

16. Min Zhou. 2001. "Straddling Different Worlds: The Acculturation of Vietnamese Refugee Children." In Ethnicities: Children of Immigrants in America, eds. Rubén G. Rumbaut and Alejandro Portes. Berkeley, CA: University of California Press, p. 198.

17. Nathan Glazer, and Daniel Patrick Moynihan. 1964 (2nd ed.) Beyond the Melting Pot: The Negroes, Puerto Ricans, Jews, Italians, and Irish of New York City. Cambridge, MA: The MIT Press.

while the latter are the only ones changing.[18] Lastly, some of the biggest criticisms of assimilation theory are that it assumes immigration is linear—point A to point B—and that immigrants want a clean break with their countries of origin.[19]

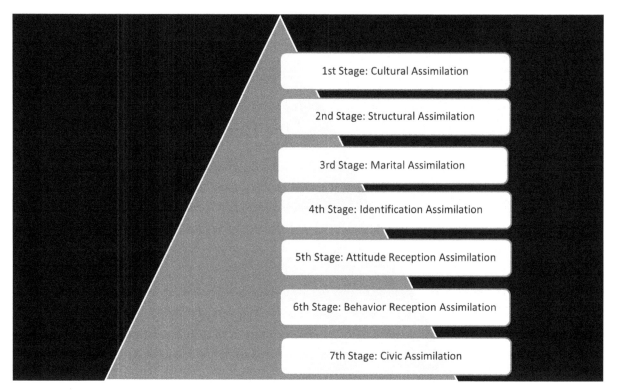

Figure 4.4   The Seven Stages of Assimilation.

Original figure based on the work of Milton Gordon; adapted from https://images.slideplayer.com/27/8965809/slides/slide_43.jpg.

Theories of assimilation eventually gave way to the idea of integration, which is the lens through which most scholars and policymakers now understand the journeys facing immigrants and refugees. Integration can be thought of as a process of "the everyday demands of fitting in."[20] This is not just about wanting to become American, but integration should be thought of as a framework where immigrants take what they need from a new society to enhance the skills they already have. This way, the lives are enriched for both the host society *and* the New American.

18. Barbara Schmitter Heisler. 2008. "The Sociology of Immigration." In Migration Theory: Talking Across Disciplines, eds. Caroline B. Brettell and James F. Hollifield. New York: Routledge, p. 83–111.

19. Douglas S. Massey, and Magaly Sánchez R. 2010. "Constructing Immigrant Identity." In Brokered Boundaries: Creating Immigrant Identity in Anti-Immigrant Times. New York: Russell Sage Foundation, p. 1–25.

20. Robert Waldinger. 2015. "The Dialectic of Emigration and Immigration." The Cross-Border Connection: Immigrants, Emigrants, and Their Homelands. Cambridge, MA: Harvard University Press, p. 50.

A great example of integration is the billion-dollar success of Hamdi Ulukaya, the founder of Chobani.[21] Ulukaya emigrated to the U.S. in 2005 from Turkey with a family background in dairy. Rather than start a new career, Ulukaya first made small-batch cheeses then bought an old Kraft yogurt factory in New York to develop Turkish-style, low-sugar yogurt. Chobani is now a massive company that pays it forward in many ways including hiring a lot of former refugees as part of a people-first company mentality. According to Ulukaya, "When we start hiring refugees, we didn't hire them because it was a refugee world. We hired them because they were people in the community, and we were growing, and we were hiring everyone. And they were in the community and we hired them."[22] This is an integration and not an assimilation story because Ulukaya used his existing skills to make cheese and yogurt and then benefited from small-business loans to start his business. The country benefits because of a healthy product that is made in the United States and by providing thousands of jobs.

Integration can also be understood in terms of naturalization, or the process of becoming a citizen. Citizenship acts like a glue that binds immigrants together more than just through certain legal protections because "it is also an invitation to participate in a system of mutual governance, and it can be an identity that provides a sense of belonging."[23] We can think of citizenship as a kind of invisible boundary that immigrants must cross to become full members of a new society.[24]

The challenge of studying immigration and refugee resettlement in the United States is understanding how newly arrived people are shaped by their host country, which is also changed in the process. Assimilation may not contend with how immigrations shape the country they now call home, but the perspective of integration does give us that theoretical space to see how immigrants' skills makes the new home better. They can retain cultures and traditions that add on to the American mosaic making our country richer in many ways. While anti-immigration anxiety never fully goes away—"whether the newcomers will fit and fears that they will undermine the basic foundations of established ways of life"[25]—is helpful to see how integration lets us imagine immigrants as contributing to the United States and not taking our culture away,

Refugee Integration in the United States and Europe

One of the immediate benefits of thinking through integration is that it is easier to craft integration outcomes. These are measurable ways of surveying and polling refugees to decide how poorly or well they are doing as new residents in their host countries. This data, in turn, helps governments, resettlement agencies, and other organizations to develop better ways of addressing the immediate and long-term needs of refugees. But, as you will learn in this section,

21. Harvard Business Review. 2022. "Chobani Founder Hamdi Ulukaya on the Journey From Abandoned Factory to Yogurt Powerhouse." April 25. https://hbr.org/2022/04/chobani-founder-hamdi-ulukaya-on-the-journey-from-abandoned-factory-to-yogurt-powerhouse
22. Ibid.
23. Irene Bloemraad. 2006. Becoming a Citizen: Incorporating Immigrants and Refugees in the United States and Canada. Berkeley, Calif.: University of California Press, p. 1.
24. T. Alexander Aleinikoff. 1995. "State-Centered Refugee Law: From Resettlement to Containment." In Mistrusting Refugees, eds. E. Valentine Daniel and John Charles Knudsen. Berkeley, CA: University of California Press, p. 267.
25. Richard Alba, and Nancy Foner. 2015. Strangers No More: Immigration and the Challenges of Integration in North America and Western Europe. Princeton, NJ: Princeton University Press, p. 2.

countries think about integration very differently and the consequence of that is a set of individualistic policies that often mean refugees must adapt quickly to different sets of expectations in different countries.

Economic integration is a key variable, for example, in Canada. Employment success is one way the country measures how well refugees are doing with finding work. But as one 2012 study showed, immigrants in Canada always trailed their Canadian-born peers in getting employed. It noted that 63.5% of immigrants who had lived in Canada for less than five years were employed, compared to 74.1% who had lived in Canada for five to 10 years, followed by 79.8% for immigrants who had lived there over a decade. But this was still lower than the 82.9% for native-born Canadians, indicating that even after 10 years, immigrants broadly still were not as employable as native-born Canadians.[26] However, one country with a more holistic approach to refugee integration is New Zealand. While employment is important, the country's official Resettlement Strategy outlines five goals of integration success:

1. "Self-sufficiency—all working-age refugees are in paid work or are supported by a family member in paid work."
2. "Participation—refugees actively participate in New Zealand life and have a strong sense of belonging here."
3. "Health and well-being—refugees and their families enjoy healthy, safe and independent lives."
4. "Education—English language skills help refugees participate in education and in daily life."
5. "Housing—refugees live in safe, secure, healthy and affordable homes, without needing government housing assistance."[27]

As we have discussed throughout this textbook, the U.S. government thinks about refugee integration through two primary lenses: learning English (but it is unclear about the level of fluency) and becoming "self-sufficient." The latter is really about job acquisition and becoming economically independent.[28] It makes sense that the U.S. prioritizes economic integration for refugees since there is a 200-year-old history of political thought about American productivity that supports this way of thinking. Alexis de Tocqueville famously described Americans as people who defined their lives based on the level of work performed, so quality of work was code for quality of life.[29]

The irony, of course, is that even though there are national-level expectations about refugee integration, it is not a national policy. In other words, Congress has not passed any law since the 1980 Refugee Act that clarifies or specifies what the federal government is looking for with regard to certain standards or outcomes for refugee integration. It has historically been left up to the states but very few have undertaken studies to look at the success and failures with refugee integration. One exception is the Colorado Department of Human Services's Refugee Integration Survey and Evaluation (RISE), which tracked refugees from Bhutan, Burma, Iraq, and Somalia for four years. The study looked at

26. Jennifer Hyndman, and Michaela Hynie. 2016. "From Newcomer to Canadian: Making Refugee Integration Work." Policy Options, May 17. https://policyoptions.irpp.org/fr/magazines/mai-2016/from-newcomer-to-canadian-making-refugee-integration-work/

27. Immigration New Zealand. 2013. Refugee Resettlement: New Zealand Resettlement Strategy, 3. https://www.immigration.govt.nz/documents/refugees/refugeeresettlementstrategy.pdf

28. Shyam K. Sriram. 2018. "The Politics of Refugee Resettlement." PhD Dissertation, University of California Santa Barbara, p. 55.

29. Ronald Takaki. 2000 (1979). Iron Cages: Race and Culture in 19th-Century America. New York: Oxford University Press, p. 73.

10 types of integration: "Economic," "Civic Engagement," "Safety and Stability," "Education and Training," "Language and Cultural Knowledge," "Social Bonding," "Social Bridging," "Children's Education," "Health and Well-Being," and "Housing."[30]

Another important study was a comparative look at Iraqi refugee experiences in Jordan versus the United States.[31] The authors interviewed Iraqis in San Diego, Detroit, and Washington, D.C., and determined that refugees were mostly initially happy with the care and reception in the United States, but were worried about the lack of long-term support (which we will tackle more in Chapter 7). According to an Iraqi widow, "I left Iraq to find security. But what kind of security is it to live in a homeless shelter?"[32]

Integration takes on a different tone when we start to look at Europe primarily because many European countries have national-level ministers and agencies in charge of integration, and there is also policy development at the level of European Union, which has its own barometer: the National Integration Evaluation Mechanism (NIEM).[33] The three broad areas of immigrant integration (and not exclusively for refugees) as defined by NIEM are "Socioeconomic Integration" (health, vocational training, employment, housing, etc.); "Legal Integration" (family unit and reunification, residency, etc.); and "Sociocultural Integration" (community building, language acquisition, children's education, etc.). This is complicated by three factors. First, not all E.U. member countries have the same understanding of integration or measure it similarly (so they have their own surveys independent of NIEM). Second, some countries monitor yearly, but not all of them make it a requirement. Third, some E.U. members believe that their own understanding of integration must take precedence over that of the European Union, or it is a loss of sovereignty.

One of the underlying challenges for European governments overseeing refugee integration is a cultural difference in what integration can and should look like. As mentioned in the last paragraph, this becomes an aggregate challenge when one country sees integration as a priority and another one does not (a similar situation arises at the state level in the United States, which we will investigate in Chapter 5). For example, Austria has a Federal Minister for Women and Integration (previously known as Minister for Foreign Affairs, Europe, and Integration). In 2018, then Minister Karin Kneissl astonished the United Nations General Assembly by first speaking fluently in Arabic before switching to other languages. Many people saw this as a strong attempt by Austria to show its commitment to diversity at the height of the Syrian refugee displacement.

30. Kit Taintor, and Gary Lichtenstein. 2016. "The Refugee Integration Survey and Evaluation (RISE) Year Five: Final Report" (A Study of Refugee Integration in Colorado), Colorado Refugee Services Program (Colorado Department of Human Services), 22 February.

31. HRI. 2009. "Refugee Crisis in America: Iraqis and Their Resettlement Experience." Georgetown University Law Center, HRI Papers & Reports. https://scholarship.law.georgetown.edu/hri_papers/4/.

32. Ibid, p. 1.

33. http://www.forintegration.eu/

QR Code 4.1

Some countries, like France and the Netherlands, insist that refugees are integrated when they share in civic values and participation with the host country. Germany believes that immigrants must adopt its national values as "universal and unquestionable." Meanwhile, Sweden has adopted more of a multicultural approach where refugee and immigrant cultural values are respect and encouraged but not at the cost of labor-market integration.[34] One study on Sweden, Norway, and Denmark noted the impossibility of conclusively saying which of the three countries was best at employment integration of refugees because of different criteria. For example, female refugees were more likely to be employed in Norway vs. Sweden but that over time, the rates of male and female refugees in Sweden finding work rose faster than Denmark or Norway.[35]

The Netherlands also emphasizes language integration as the most important way for new immigrants to become Dutch even though it is just one of the many NIEM outcomes. The government has made it a requisite for citizenship (with language classes paid by the government),[36] but anyone wishing to move to the Netherlands must pass an exam before emigrating (with only a few countries exempt).[37] Greece also emphasizes language as the primary pathway to integration, but the government has struggled to balance its desire for immigrants to retain their cultural heritage while simultaneously learning Greek to become a more fully accepted part of their society. Government-run language classes are available across the country, but it is still difficult to get new immigrants and refugees to voluntarily learn Greek.[38] An additional challenge is that many of those seeking asylum often lack

34. Irina Isaakyan. 2016. "Integration Paradigms in Europe and North America." In The Routledge Handbook of Immigration and Refugee Studies, ed. Anna Triandafyllidou. London: Routledge, p. 172.

35. Kristian Tronstad, , Vilde Hernes, Pernilla Anderson Joona, and Jacob Arendt. 2019. "Unique Study Compares How Denmark, Norway and Sweden Integrate Refugees." Nordic Labour Journal, April 29. http://www.nordiclabourjournal.org/i-fokus/in-focus-2019/inclusion/article.2019-04-29.3965125181

36. Masja van Meeteren, Sanne van de Pol, Rianne Dekker, Godfried Engbersen, and Erik Snel. 2013. "Destination Netherlands: History of Immigration and Immigration Policy in the Netherlands." In Immigrants: Acculturation, Socioeconomic Challenges, and Cultural Psychology, ed. Judy Ho. New York: Nova Publishers, p. 127 – 129.

37. Sriram. 2018. p. 54.

38. Eleni Griva, and Eugenia Panitsides. 2013. "Immigration and Education: Policy and Practices for Integration and Inclusion in the Greek Context." In Immigrants: Acculturation, Socioeconomic Challenges, and Cultural Psychology, ed. Judy Ho. New York: Nova Publishers, p. 265–279.

primary language literacy or their languages are not recognized or supported by humanitarian aid workers, resulting in multiple communication barriers.[39]

The Question: Should refugee integration be national policy in the United States? Is the federal government responsible for refugee integration or should that be left to individual states or agencies?

Case Studies in Refugee Resettlement

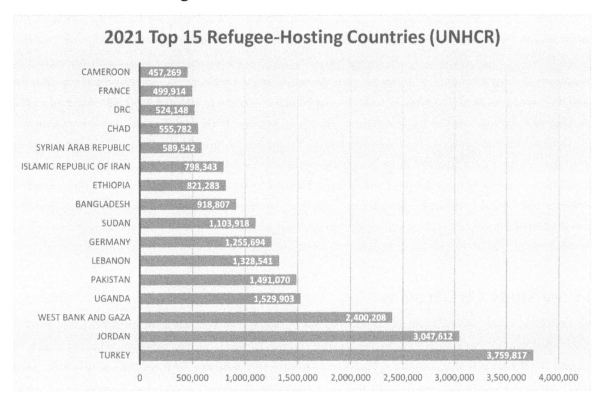

Figure 4.5   Top Refugee-Hosting Countries in 2021.

Data Source: https://data.worldbank.org/indicator/SM.POP.REFG?name_desc=false

We began this chapter with a discussion about how countries are often forced into unlikely roles as refugee caregivers when neighboring instability, famine, war, and persecution force people to flee. When they cross an international border and register with the UNHCR, they become refugees (although as we have learned, not all refugees are given official recognition and status). There is so much to learn from Figure 4.5, but as we can see, most of the countries in the top 15 for accepting refugees are in extremely volatile areas. In the concluding section of this chapter, you will learn about refugee resettlement in three countries: Chad, Germany, and Bangladesh. Each country is presented as a brief case study that highlights a bit of its history and how refugees are perceived (positively and negatively). These countries were also chosen because each is associated with different communities of displaced people.

39. Nada Ghandour-Demiri. 2017. "Language and Comprehension Barriers in Greece's Migration Crisis." Translators Without Borders, June, p 7–8.

a) Case Study #1: Chad

The United Nations Development Program (UNDP) uses a measurement known as the Human Development Index (HDI) to calculate global poverty. The HDI score ranges from 0 to 1.000 and is calculated based on the life expectancy, gross national product per capita, years of schooling, and other variables. The highest country score is 0.962 for Switzerland and the lowest score is 0.385 for the Republic of South Sudan. Chad's 2021 HDI score is 0.394, the second lowest among all countries.[40]

So, why is a poor, landlocked country in Africa also home to over 550,000 refugees? Part of the reason is Chad's location next to the Central African Republic (CAR), Niger, Libya, South Sudan, Sudan, and Nigeria, "instability on every border."[41] Chad also has a sizable population of internally displaced persons due to intertribal conflict and violence near the Nigerian border with Boko Haram. According to the UNHCR, "the Government of Chad has kept its asylum space open. As of December 31, 2022, the population of concern to UNHCR was 1,080,568, of which 55% were refugees and 1% asylum seekers, 35% internally displaced persons (IDPs), and 9% other persons of concern."[42]

Despite its extreme poverty, Chad has a surprisingly robust commitment to accepting political asylees and is a major regional and African leader in this capacity, which provides food for thought about the relationship between infrastructure and capacity to receive those seeking help. The country is part of the Comprehensive Refugee Response Framework and Global Compact on Refugees and provides a number of resources for political asylees, including access to naturalization; health clinics; schools and colleges with scholarships just for refugees; and land for refugees to establish farms.[43] Most refugees are from Sudan, so Chad's refugee camps are mostly on its eastern border.[44]

b) Case Study #2: Germany

Germany's history has a direct impact on its status as one of the most welcoming countries in the world today for refugees. Between 2015 and 2016, the country became a haven for over a million refugees combined, which was a massive boost over past years' asylum applications. As Figure 4.6 illustrates, there were more first-time asylum applications in 2015 alone than the previous five years combined! According to one source, Germany saw over a million Ukrainian refugees in 2022 alone (who were immediately given temporary residency and did not have to apply for asylum) and an additional 244,000 other asylum applications.[45] Germany is also unique because it is a major refugee host and the second-largest donor to the United Nations High Commissioner on Refugees.[46]

40. UNDP. 2021. "Human Development Index (HDI)." United Nations Development Programme. https://hdr.undp.org/data-center/human-development-index#/indicies/HDI

41. Geopolitical Monitor. 2021. "Post-Déby Chad: Instability on Every Border." Situation Reports, April 20. https://www.geopoliticalmonitor.com/post-deby-chad-instability-on-every-border/

42. UNHCR. 2023. "Chad: Strategy 2023." https://reporting.unhcr.org/operational/operations/chad

43. Integral Human Development. "Country Profiles: Chad." https://migrants-refugees.va/it/wp-content/uploads/sites/3/2022/01/2021-CP-Chad.pdf

44. HIAS. 2023. "Chad." https://hias.org/where/chad/

45. Associated Press. 2023. "Number of Refugees, Asylum-Seekers Increase in Germany." *U.S. News & World Report*, January 11. https://www.usnews.com/news/business/articles/2023-01-11/numbers-of-refugees-asylum-seekers-increase-in-germany

46. UNHCR. 2023. "Germany." Global Focus: UNHCR Operations Worldwide. https://reporting.unhcr.org/donors/germany.

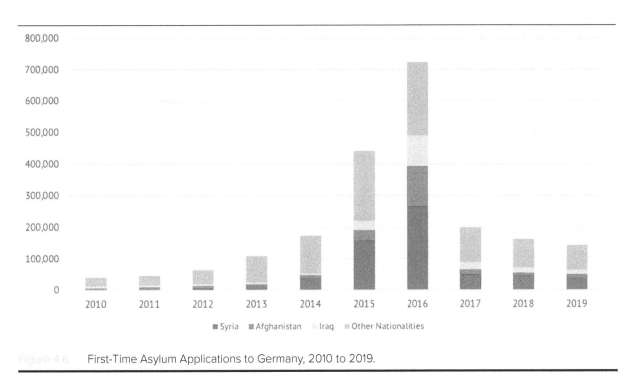

800,000
700,000
600,000
500,000
400,000
300,000
200,000
100,000
0

2010 2011 2012 2013 2014 2015 2016 2017 2018 2019

■ Syria ■ Afghanistan ▨ Iraq ▨ Other Nationalities

Figure 4.6   First-Time Asylum Applications to Germany, 2010 to 2019.

Ninety years later, the horrors of the Nazi Party, the Holocaust, and World War II (which you read about in Chapter 2) continue to haunt Germany. There are now specific phrases in the German language that are frequently invoked by everyday people and politicians to constantly remind citizens of their responsibilities. The phrase Täter means "criminal" although it is often used to mean "perpetrator" in the context of Nazis.[47] The opposite of Täter is the German word Opfer, which now means "victim" (although at one time meant "sacrificial").[48] Initially, people were aware of their guilt as Täter, as perpetrators. The collective memory of the atrocities of the Third Reich, however, has changed drastically over time as the initial identification with the perpetrators has shifted to a general identification with the victims.[49] Another phrase that has grown in popularity since the 1950s in Germany is Vergangenheitsbewältigung, which translates as "a coming to terms or reconciliation with the past."[50] Former German President Richard von Weizsäcker once said, "those who close their eyes to the past become blind to the present."[51] Last, Germans also now commonly use the phrase Willkommenskultur, which roughly translates as a

47. Etymologisches Wörterbuch des Deutschen. 2023. "Täter." https://www.dwds.de/wb/etymwb/t%C3%A4ter

48. Etymologisches Wörterbuch des Deutschen. 2023. "Opfer." https://www.dwds.de/wb/etymwb/opfer

49. Personal Interview with Ida Segmüller, 2023. Zoom (unpublished).

50. Ibid.

51. Ulrike Jureit. 2019. "Gefühlte Opfer: Illusionen Der Vergangenheitsbewältigung." S: I.M.O.N. Shoah: Intervention. Methods. Documentation 1 (2) (August): p. 82 https://simon.vwi.ac.at/index.php/simon/article/view/139

welcoming culture. It depicts a host society that welcomes the arrival of new people and has been used frequently in Germany since 2015 as the country welcomed Syrian refugees, among many, and, more recently, Ukrainians.[52]

c) Case Study #3: Bangladesh

The third and final case study in this chapter belongs to Bangladesh, the eighth most populated country in the world with over 167 million people.[53] As we saw earlier in Figure 4.5, Bangladesh is currently ranked ninth globally for the number of refugees within its borders. Almost all of those refugees are Rohingya Muslims from Rakhine State in Burma (Myanmar), who started fleeing Burma in 2017 due to ethnic violence and genocide from the Buddhist Burmese Government. Thousands of Rohingya were slaughtered, raped, and driven from their homes by the Tatmadaw, or military, who had persecuted the Rohingya for decades but only took over the country in a 2021 coup.[54]

Most of the Rohingya refugees live in Cox's Bazar, the largest refugee camp in the world.[55] Over a hundred public and private nongovernmental organizations (NGOs) from Bangladesh, the United Nations, and other countries have established services in Cox's Bazar.[56] There have been many success stories, including resources for COVID, reproductive health, mental health, and entrepreneurship. However, it is well documented that life for the Rohingya continues to be very hard in this refugee camp. A deadly fire in March 2021, determined to be arson, wiped out 2,800 shelters and displaced 15,000 Rohingya within the camp.[57] There are daily threats of violence, particularly sexual harassment, intimidation, and rape for the Rohingya women and girls who form 52% of the residents.[58]

But what makes the Rohingya's situation even more difficult than that of the refugees in Chad or Germany is that the right of return does not exist, and naturalization is not an option. The Burmese Military Government currently in power does not want the Rohingya to return to their homes and repatriate.[59] While historical records

52. Shyam K. Sriram., Giuliano Espino, Ida Segmüller, Bree Kruszka, and Leah Rozbicki. "Political Culture May Be Why Wyoming Is the Only State Not to Resettle Refugees," United States Politics and Policy Blog, London School of Economics, July 3. https://blogs.lse.ac.uk/usappblog/2023/07/03/political-culture-may-be-why-wyoming-is-the-only-state-not-to-resettle-refugees/

53. US Census Bureau. 2023. "U.S. Census Bureau Current Population." https://www.census.gov/popclock/print.php?component=counter

54. Megan Rodgers. 2022. "Perpetrators in Power: Growing Mass Atrocity Risk in Post-Coup Burma." United States Holocaust Memorial Museum (Announcements and Recent Analysis), January 28. https://www.ushmm.org/genocide-prevention/blog/perpetrators-in-power

55. Danish Refugee Council. 2023. "Rohingya in Bangladesh: The World's Largest Refugee Camp." https://help.drc.ngo/en/how-we-work/life-as-a-refugee/rohingya-in-bangladesh-the-world-s-largest-refugee-camp/

56. Afshan Paarlberg, Ronia Hawash, and Shyam K. Sriram. 2023. "Voiceless and Stateless: Competing Expectations Between Rohingya Refugees and NGOs in Cox's Bazar, Bangladesh" VOLUNTAS, p. 1 – 12.

57. Kelly Ng. 2021. "Rohingya Camp Fire Was 'Planned Sabotage'—Investigators." BBC News, March 13. https://www.bbc.com/news/world-asia-64935831

58. Kathy Win. 2023. "Cox's Bazaar: Insecurity, Criminality, and Rohingya Women." London School of Economics, February 6. https://blogs.lse.ac.uk/southasia/2023/02/06/coxs-bazaar-insecurity-criminality-and-rohingya-women/

59. USCIRF. 2023. "USCIRF Calls for Accountability of Tatmadaw at Two Year Anniversary of Coup in Burma." United States Commission on International Religious Freedom, February 1. https://www.uscirf.gov/news-room/releases-statements/uscirf-calls-accountability-tatmadaw-two-year-anniversary-coup-burma

show the presence of Rohingya in Burma as early as the fifteenth century, Burma has never accorded them citizenship.[60]

Bangladesh also has a unique set of politics and circumstances surrounding its refugee policy. The country is not a signatory to the 1951 Refugee Convention but has a robust and supportive relationship with the UNHCR and other refugee-related NGOs.[61] And yet, despite these efforts, the Rohingya can never become Bangladeshi citizens because there is no process of naturalization for immigrants and refugees. In fact, being born in Bangladesh does not guarantee citizenship unless it is through marriage or having one native parent.[62]

List of Key Takeaways

- One of the most unique features of refugee admissions in the United States is the role of private, mostly Christian, nonprofit organizations working as resettlement partners with the federal government.
- This has added significance because integration is not a federal priority or policy in the United States. That responsibility falls on these private partners and states.
- Americans love to talk about the history of the country as a dream for immigrants, but current realities are starkly different. The United States is not even in the top fifteen refugee-hosting countries.
- A major reason is that political rhetoric or speech about immigrants has changed drastically in the United States. Immigration is now framed as an issue about who should be allowed into the country or what kind of person is best for the United States.
- For decades, the key theory to explain immigration was assimilation, which was a slow process of an immigrant losing their cultural and political identity to become American and cut ties with their past. The goal of assimilation was Eurocentric: to identify with values associated with white, Christian Americans of European descent.
- The theory of integration has now replaced assimilation as a better predictor of immigrant and refugee success in the United States. Integration allows the immigrant to use their extant skills to meet the needs of the labor market, for example, so that the host society is also improved by the arrival of the New American.
- Integration provides space for the host society to be changed as much as the immigrant.
- Most countries have adopted refugee integration outcomes to determine what makes good policy when it comes to easing the transition for refugees into new societies. These can be measured in many different ways, including language acquisition, job training, school attendance, etc.

60. Christopher M. Faulkner, and Samuel Schiffer. 2019. "Rohingya Refugees in Bangladesh: How the Absence of Citizenship Rights Acts as a Barrier to Successful Repatriation." London School of Economics, June 12. https://blogs.lse.ac.uk/southasia/2019/06/12/rohingya-refugees-in-bangladesh-how-a-lack-citizenship-rights-are-a-barrier-to-successful-repatriation/
61. Naureen Rahim. 2023. "Bangladesh and the 1951 Refugee Convention." Refugee Law Initiative (RLI) Blog (School of Advanced Study, University of London), February 6. https://rli.blogs.sas.ac.uk/2023/02/06/bangladesh-and-the-1951-refugee-convention/
62. Sajeeb Wazed. 2018. "Why Bangladesh Cannot Accept All the Rohingya." The Diplomat, January 19. https://thediplomat.com/2018/01/why-bangladesh-cannot-accept-all-the-rohingya/

- Chad, Bangladesh, and Germany have unique experiences as refugee-hosting countries. Chad is one of the poorest countries in the world but borders a very unstable region in Africa, so displaced people are constantly seeking asylum in Chad. However, the country offers many programs to help displaced people succeed.
- Germany has become one of the top destinations for asylum seekers since 2015. Its World War II-era participation in the Holocaust continues to linger over the culture and citizens, who still feel responsible for the Nazi regime. This has made Germans keen on reconciling their past with current actions, like welcoming refugees.
- Almost all the refugees in Bangladesh are Rohingya Muslims from bordering Burma (also known as Myanmar). The Rohingya are caught in an impossible situation because Bangladesh does not allow naturalization (a process to become a citizen), and Burma does not want the Rohingya to return.

Chapter Review Questions

1. **What** can we infer from Figures 4.1 and 4.2 and the map of resettlement organizations?
   a. Some states have only one resettlement site and agency handling those needs.
   b. Wyoming has no resettlement program.
   c. There are more resettlement sites in the Midwest and East Coast states compared to the rest of the country.
   d. All of the above (CORRECT)
2. **How** does the huge rise in Christian **conversion** and practice among Hmong Americans relate to the structure of refugee resettlement?
3. **Why** would President Trump's repeated references to "build the wall" qualify as dog-whistle politics?
4. **Demonstrate** an understanding of integration by drawing on the life of Hamdi Ulukaya.
5. **Choose** ONE possible weakness with Canada's economic integration goals for refugees. Why would the rate of employment be a poor determinant of integration?
6. **Which** of the following countries has a mandatory language exam that must be passed *before* emigrating to ensure greater integration into the new country?
   a. United States
   b. Australia
   c. Ghana
   d. The Netherlands (CORRECT)
7. **Summarize** the reasons why Chad has such a robust refugee program despite its country being one of the poorest in the world.

8. **What** is the majority religion in Burma?
   a. Buddhism (CORRECT)
   b. Islam
   c. Christianity
   d. Hinduism

Critical Thinking Questions

1. **Recommend** a policy decision to the federal government with a holistic understanding of refugee integration in mind (like New Zealand).
2. **Elaborate** on the concept of white saviorism, and **choose** one example related to refugee resettlement from this chapter (or elsewhere in the textbook).
3. **Explain** this statement: "The Hmong are a stateless nationality most often associated with Laos and Cambodia but are often neither Laotian nor Cambodian by ethnicity."
4. **Construct** arguments to support and oppose the inclusion of an English language requirement for U.S. birthright citizenship.
5. **Adapt** the German phrases Vergangenheitsbewältigung (reconciliation with the past) and Willkommenskultur (welcoming culture) to a country or political situation outside of Europe. How can these concepts be applied in other contexts?

CHAPTER 5

Federalism and State Policies

Opening Vignette

On September 26, 2019, President Trump signed Executive Order 13888, which made it mandatory for the federal government to seek consent from state and local governments before resettling refugees in those areas. According to the order,

> In resettling refugees into American communities, it is the policy of the United States to cooperate and consult with State and local governments, to take into account the preferences of State governments, and to provide a pathway for refugees to become self-sufficient … Within 90 days of the date of this order, the Secretary of State and the Secretary of Health and Human Services shall develop and implement a process to determine whether the State and locality both consent, in writing, to the resettlement of refugees within the State and locality, before refugees are resettled within that State and locality under the Program.[1]

This was a tectonic policy shift that caught many off guard; for the first time in our history, the president had devolved refugee resettlement from the national to the state level.[2] Legal scholars also questioned if EO 13888 actually diminished state power (rather than boosting it): "the order requires resettlement agencies to seek the consent not only of state governments in refugee resettlement, but also of local governments. That means, even if a state were to consent to refugee resettlement within its borders, a resettlement agency still must gain the consent of specific local governments within that state for full compliance with the EO."[3]

Appomattox County (Virginia)[4] became the first county in the country in December 2019 to take a legislative

1. https://www.presidency.ucsb.edu/documents/executive-order-13888-enhancing-state-and-local-involvement-refugee-resettlement
2. "Devolution is the transfer or delegation of power from a central government to a subnational, local authority." Wex Definitions Team. 2021. "Devolution." Legal Information Institute (Cornell University). https://www.law.cornell.edu/wex/devolution
3. Meryl Chertoff, and William Rice. 2019. "Does President Trump's Refugee Executive Order Violate State Sovereignty?" The Georgetown Project on State and Local Government Policy and Law (SALPAL), Georgetown University. https://www.law.georgetown.edu/salpal/does-president-trumps-refugee-executive-order-violate-state-sovereignty/
4. Elizabeth Tyree, Valencia Jones, and Kalcey Brown. 2019. "Appomattox Co. Passes Resolution Refusing to Become a Refugee Sanctuary." ABC 13 News, December 16. https://wset.com/news/local/appomattox-co-to-vote-on-resolution-refusing-to-become-refugee-sanctuary

step inspired by President Trump's executive order. Their council voted against the county becoming a refugee sanctuary. Burleigh County (North Dakota)[5] acted next, followed by Beltrami County (Minnesota) in January 2020.[6]

While Trump's order continued to ripple across states municipalities, it was challenged immediately by refugee resettlement organizations and state and local governments in court. By January 2021, the United States 4th Circuit Court of Appeals affirmed a lower court ruling and blocked the executive order indefinitely because it would "violate the carefully crafted scheme for resettling refugees that Congress established in the Refugee Act."[7] On February 4, 2021, two weeks after taking office, President Joe Biden revoked EO 13888.[8]

Figure 5.1   President Biden signs executive orders on his first day in office.

Office of President Joe Biden, https://commons.wikimedia.org/wiki/File:Joe_Biden_signs_a_bill.jpg, 2022.

5. Kelly Mena. 2019. "North Dakota County Approves Refugee Resettlement Under Terms of Trump Executive Order." CNN, December 10. https://www.cnn.com/2019/12/09/politics/north-dakota-refugees-burleigh-county/index.html

6. Jon Collins, and John Enger. 2020. "Beltrami Co. Becomes First in State to Reject Refugee Resettlement." MPR News, January 7. https://www.mprnews.org/story/2020/01/07/beltrami-co-rejects-refugee-resettlement.

7. HIAS v. Trump. 2021. https://www.ca4.uscourts.gov/opinions/201160.P.pdf

8. Joseph Biden. 2021. "Executive Order on Rebuilding and Enhancing Programs to Resettle Refugees and Planning for the Impact of Climate Change on Migration." White House Briefing Room (Presidential Actions), February 4. https://www.whitehouse.gov/briefing-room/presidential-actions/2021/02/04/executive-order-on-rebuilding-and-enhancing-programs-to-resettle-refugees-and-planning-for-the-impact-of-climate-change-on-migration/

Introduction to the Chapter

Several countries have federal systems where power is shared between states and the national government (though most countries are unitary where power is centralized and where there is often minimal variation across the land). What makes American federalism so special is that our Constitution contains two civil liberties captured under the Ninth- and Tenth Amendments that essentially allow states to "create their own statutes and policies as long as they are not in conflict with the U.S. Constitution or congressional law."[9] In other words, if a power has not exclusively been granted to the federal government, some might say those powers and policies are up to the states and the people. But this is tricky because there are many policies not mentioned in the Constitution that were not even fathomable in the eighteenth century when the Constitution was first written.

The Question: Should states be responsible for some public policies and not others, or should the federal government be in control of all policymaking?

One of those policies is refugee resettlement. As you learned with the opening vignette about President Trump's failed executive order, refugee admissions and resettlement are primarily federal policies implemented through elaborate and complex partnerships with private refugee resettlement organizations (RROs); city, county, and state governments; and a lot of other stakeholders and actors.

In this chapter, we will turn our attention to states to understand how the subnational governments in the United States have historically responded to the informal and formal refugee program (before and since the 1980 Refugee Act). State politics is a fascinating field of study for precisely the reasons laid out above; the same state may have once been very supportive of refugees and is now much less so (although we will analyze opinion and polling data in Chapter 6).

Learning Objectives

Reading this chapter will enable readers to:

- **Interpret** the stages of resettlement policy implementation.
- **Assess** refugee resettlement frameworks across the United States.
- **Construct** an overview of the factors affecting states' refugee policies.

Federalism and the Challenges of Policy Implementation

Political culture is a concept relating to the unique features of a country or political space (state or institution). It includes "the ways in which traditions and cultural values create that country's specific political system. A country's particular combination of history, geography, religious practices, conflict, and other identities contributes to creating

---

9. Ibid, p. 207.

its specific political culture."[10] There are a lot of features of American political culture that are unique, but one that stands out is federalism.

Federalism shapes the lives of every American citizen, resident, and even tourist whether they want to believe it or not. Let's reflect on COVID policies a few years ago. The State of Washington was one of the first in the country to declare a public health crisis. On February 29, 2020, Governor Jay Inslee said the emergency demanded "common-sense, proactive measures to ensure the health and safety of those who live in Washington state."[11] However, Idaho, which borders Washington to the east, never saw COVID as a crisis. Rather, as Governor Brad Little announced on March 8, 2022, "I kept Idaho open, banned vaccine passports, never issued mandates for vaccines or masks, and successfully challenged Biden's overreaching vaccine mandates in court."[12] And then, one state over to the east, Montana again took a more intense approach to halt the spread the COVID. Governor Steve Bullock set the lofty goal of testing 60,000 Montanans a month by June 2020 and had, at the time, "the lowest coronavirus infection rate in the nation and among the lowest hospitalizations and deaths."[13] All of this was also under the context of federal vaccination mandates that many states found too intrusive and limiting.

Federalism in the United States, as mentioned in the last section, has created an extraordinary system where policies can vary *within* a state, between states (even those that border each other), and, in some cases, vary between a state and the federal government. One of the factors that makes resettlement policy and implementation so complex is that ***federal programs are often administered by states and local governments***. For example, the Supplemental Nutrition Assistance Program (SNAP) now serves 42 million Americans (up from 36 million in 2019).[14] By budget and scope, SNAP is the largest program in the country to alleviate hunger. According to recent research,

> Like many federal programs, SNAP is implemented through the states, which pay approximately half of its administrative costs. Moreover, while the federal government sets SNAP eligibility rules and benefit levels, states are granted some flexibility in program implementation, ranging from the design of processes for benefit application and renewal to the stringency of work rules for able-bodied adults.[15]

As you can imagine, SNAP benefits not only vary by state but have disproportionate effects based on the cost of living, unemployment, level of food security, etc. California implements SNAP through its own CalFresh program,

10. Shyam K. Sriram. 2022. "Civil Rights." Introduction to Political Science, eds. Mark Carl Rom, Masaki Hidaka, and Rachel Bzostek Walker. OpenStax (Houston: Rice University), p. 206.

11. The Office of the Governor. 2020. "Inslee Issues COVID-19 Emergency Proclamation." February 29. https://governor.wa.gov/news/2020/inslee-issues-covid-19-emergency-proclamation

12. Office of the Governor. 2022. "Public Health Disaster Emergency Declaration to End April 15." March 8. https://gov.idaho.gov/pressrelease/public-health-disaster-emergency-declaration-to-end-april-15/

13. Kirk Siegler. 2020. "Steve Bullock's COVID-19 Response May Boost His Senate Run in Montana." NPR, June 25. https://www.npr.org/2020/06/25/882311863/on-the-covid-19-campaign-trail-montanas-gov-steve-bullock-may-be-getting-a-boost

14. Chris Edwards. 2023. "SNAP Spending Doubles to $127 Billion." CATO Institute (CATO at Liberty), April 3. https://www.cato.org/blog/snap-spending-doubles-127-billion

15. Giuliano Espino, and Christopher Bosso. 2019. "Policy Innovation in the U.S. States: Gubernatorial v. Local Experimentation in Administering the Supplemental Nutrition Assistance Program." (Unpublished).

serving 12% of its population, or one in eight residents. In the program, 40% of recipients are in working families and, on average, CalFresh benefits average about $196 per household member per month.[16] By contrast, 25% of New Mexico residents receive SNAP: one in four people. In New Mexico, 47% are working families, and the average household benefit is $182 per month.[17]

Refugee resettlement policy has its own vehicle for implementation, which is a relationship between the federal government, states, counties, and private, nonprofit organizations (national and regional offices). Let us look at the state of Illinois as an example of how its program runs, which also illustrates how confusing refugee policy implementation can be even for experts! First, Illinois is one of the states that oversees its refugee resettlement program. Two agencies—the Illinois Department of Human Services and the Bureau of Refugee and Immigrant Services—handle most of the oversight. However, the state's refugee-related employment and social services programs are administered by a private agency, the Jewish Federation of Metropolitan Chicago.[18]

The Jewish Federation and the State of Illinois then work with thirteen service providers across the state, not just in Chicago, to make sure refugees get all the services they are legally mandated to receive. Some of these providers include World Relief in Chicago, DuPage/Aurora, and Moline; Ethiopian Community Association of Chicago; Heartland Alliance Health; Chicago Public Schools; and the Iraqi Mutual Aid Society. There are also five community clinics statewide administered largely by county departments of health.[19]

Admission and resettlement have approximately five stages (whose funding structures will be discussed more in Chapter 7):

1. Every year, the President of the United States informs Congress on the refugee ceiling (the maximum number of refugees he wants to accept into the country).
2. That number is relayed to the United Nations High Commissioner for Refugees (UNHCR), which administers the global refugee registration program.
3. The United States Government signs a memorandum of understanding (MoU) with a national refugee resettlement organization (RRO). Part of that MoU includes a specific reference to the cost of resettling each refugee.
4. The national RRO works with its regional affiliates and offices to decide how many refugees will move to which cities and states.
5. The local office/agency takes on the responsibility of meeting the refugee family at the airport, helping it adjust to life in the United States, finding employment, etc.

16. Lauren Hall, and Catlin Nchako. 2023. "A Closer Look at Who Benefits from SNAP: State-by-State Fact Sheets." Center on Budget and Policy Priorities (Food Assistance), February 13. https://www.cbpp.org/research/food-assistance/a-closer-look-at-who-benefits-from-snap-state-by-state-fact-sheets#California

17. Lauren Hall, and Catlin Nchako. 2023. "A Closer Look at Who Benefits from SNAP: State-by-State Fact Sheets." Center on Budget and Policy Priorities (Food Assistance), February 13. https://www.cbpp.org/research/food-assistance/a-closer-look-at-who-benefits-from-snap-state-by-state-fact-sheets#New_Mexico

18. Illinois Department of Human Services. 2023. "Refugee Program." https://www.dhs.state.il.us/page.aspx?item=137611.

19. Ibid.

Resettlement and Federalism[20,21]

- 30,993 refugees have already been resettled through the end of January 2024.
- That is 24.79% of the 125,000 refugee ceiling designated by President Biden and Congress for the year.
- Mississippi accepted just 12 refugees (four from Eritrea, six from Nicaragua, and two from Sudan). At the other end of the spectrum, California accepted 2,374 refugees representing 31 countries.
- Texas has consistently been among the top three states since 1975 for refugees.[22]
- The top refugee receiving states were Texas, New York, California, Kentucky (1,886), and Pennsylvania (1,718).
- The top country of origin so far in 2024 is the Democratic Republic of the Congo (DRC), with 7,408 arrivals or 23 percent of all refugees so far this year.
- The DRC is followed by Syria (5,837), Afghanistan (4,626), Burma (2,073), Guatemala (1,325), Ukraine (1,020), and Venezuela (1,274).

State Resettlement Frameworks

The primary distinction in resettlement policy and implementation is the degree to which a state is involved in managing the program. Private, refugee resettlement organizations (RROs)—mostly Christian-based, as discussed at the beginning of Chapter 4—have offices and partners in the states where they either work in tandem with state governments and agencies to carry out resettlement or carry out resettlement themselves. When states decide they no longer want to administer resettlement, they designate a private resettlement organization to carry out that role, also known as the replacement designee (RD).[23]

20. Office of Admissions—Refugee Processing Center. 2024. "Summary of Refugee Admissions as of 31-January-2024." Bureau of Population, Refugees, and Migration (Department of State). https://www.wrapsnet.org/documents/PRM%20Refugee%20Admissions%20Report%20as%20of%2031%20Jan%202024.xlsx

21. Office of Admissions—Refugee Processing Center. 2024. "Refugee Arrivals by State and Nationality Fiscal Year 2024." Bureau of Population, Refugees, and Migration (Department of State). https://www.wrapsnet.org/documents/Refugee%20Arrivals%20by%20State%20and%20Nationality%20as%20of%2031%20Jan%202024.pdf.

22. https://www.refugeeresettlementdata.com/

23. Office of Refugee Resettlement. 2022. "Replacement Designees (Policy Letter 18-03.)" Administration for Children & Families, March 1st (originally published June 26, 2018). https://www.acf.hhs.gov/orr/policy-guidance/replacement-designees

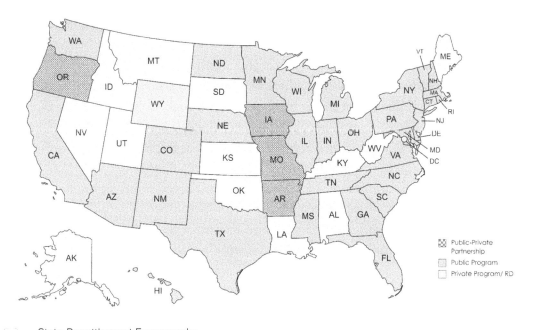

Figure 5.2   State Resettlement Frameworks.

Forty-nine of the 50 states have state refugee coordinators (SRCs), but not all SRCs are created equal; their workload and scope of involvement is directly proportional to the kind of resettlement framework in their state. This is a nuanced discussion because there are some states that administer and oversee the resettlement program but whose SRCs have little oversight and prefer to let the private agencies take the lead. One such state is Georgia, whose refugee coordinator is not as involved in the day-to-day operations as one might think. Implementation power is truly in the hands of the RRO caseworkers and managers of agencies, like Lutheran Services, World Relief, Catholic Charities, and Refugee Resettlement and Immigration Services of Atlanta (RRISA).[24]

California, on the other hand, is vastly different. This is also a state with public management of its resettlement program, but the state refugee coordinator there was deeply involved in every aspect of helping refugees succeed. One unique feature of California's program is that county-level coordinators had more discretion about the kinds of services they could provide at the local level (something rarely seen in other states).[25]

Most Americans also do not realize how these programs are funded. Imagine "each refugee has a certain dollar sign attached to his or her head; that figure is the estimate of how much it will cost over 180 days (the average time of resettlement services) to provide for that refugee." That amount is then multiplied, and the funding for that group of refugees is paid for by the federal government, which gives the money to the national RRO, which then distributes it to the local affiliates.[26] Current allocation per refugee, according to the Refugee Admissions Program (RAP) under

24. Shyam Krishnan Sriram. 2020. "The Hierarchical Integration Model of Refugee Resettlement: A Comparative Analysis of Georgia and California." The Journal of Political Science, 48: 7–29, p. 20.

25. Ibid, p. 21.

26. Ibid, p. 16.

the Department of State, is $2,375. However, if the costs exceed the allocation, the refugee resettlement organization must make up the balance.[27]

One unique program used in 13 states and one county (San Diego, California) is Wilson-Fish, named for two U.S. senators who authored a new policy as an alternative to the traditional funding approach for refugee resettlement. Instead of federal funding administered by the Office of Refugee Resettlement (ORR) to several public and private agencies helping refugees in each state, the Wilson-Fish program provides federal ORR funding directly to only *one agency* in each state. That agency is responsible for redistributing the grant funds as seen fit to help refugees attain self-sufficiency quicker.[28] ORR lists three formal purposes of the program:

1. Increase refugee prospects for early employment and self-sufficiency.
2. Promote coordination among voluntary resettlement agencies and service providers.
3. Ensure that refugee assistance programs exist in every state where refugees are resettled.[29]

What makes Wilson-Fish so fascinating is that, in some ways, it allows state governments to "bypass" working directly with the federal government so that a private local agency is the point person for all refugee work.[30] A downside to the program, however, is that self-sufficiency is motivated by the idea that it is a short- and not long-term goal so that refugees often get work but in entry-level jobs that may not meet their qualifications. One policy recommendation is,

> An emphasis on integration should immediately follow self-sufficiency; the program should not be satisfied when clients are simply financially independent. If the program acknowledges from the beginning that goals beyond entry-level employment exist, clients will be prepared to work toward integration."[31]

Recent analysis has confirmed that Wilson-Fish states between 2005 and 2019 performed better than other states. Employees and caseworkers in Wilson-Fish states had lower caseloads, which correlated to stronger outcomes, including number of refugees finding employment.[32] There are also encouraging signs of immediate consequences

27. Stella Chávez. 2023. "What to Know About Refugee Services of Texas's Closure." KERA: News for North Texas, June 1. https://www.keranews.org/news/2023-06-01/what-to-know-about-refugee-services-of-texas-closure

28. Raquel Jae Rosenbloom. 2023. Comparing the Effectiveness of Refugee Resettlement Models: An Analysis of the Wilson-Fish Alternative Model and Employment Outcomes." Master's Thesis, Georgetown University, p. 1. https://repository.library.georgetown.edu/bitstream/handle/10822/1082708/Rosenbloom_georgetown_0076M_15446.pdf

29. Office of Refugee Resettlement. 2020. "About Wilson/Fish." Administration for Children & Families, April 6. https://www.acf.hhs.gov/archive/orr/programs/wilson-fish/about.

30. Austin Anderson. 2017. "The Administration of Refugee Resettlement in the United States: An Analysis of the Wilson-Fish Alternative Program." Sentinels Fellowship, Williams College, p. 2.

31. Ibid, p. 22.

32. Rosenbloom. 2023. p. 31–33.

for refugees' benefit when a state switches to the Wilson-Fish program. One example is Tennessee, whose refugee job retention skyrocketed from 20% to 50% in one year.[33]

Figure 5.3   Wilson-Fish States.

States' Rights

- Doctrine emphasizes the supremacy and centrality of states' policies and their residents' needs over that of the national government.
- States' rights are most often associated with the States Rights Democratic Party, whose 1948 presidential platform emphasized "the segregation of the races and the racial integrity of each race … [and opposition to] the action of the Democratic Convention in sponsoring a civil rights program calling for the elimination of segregation."[34]

33. Ibid, p. 33–34.

34. American Presidency Project. 1948. "Platform of the States Rights Democratic Party." Minor/Third Party Platforms. Gerhard Peters and John T. Woolley. https://www.presidency.ucsb.edu/node/273454

- In more recent years, however, the states' rights movement has gained support due to loss of faith in national institutions; "reinvigorating federalism may provide better solutions to many of the problems that the federal government has tackled unsuccessfully."[35]
- One challenge to this is Article VI of the U.S. Constitution. The Supremacy Clause mandates the "federal constitution, and federal law generally, take precedence over state laws, and even state constitutions. It prohibits states from interfering with the federal government's exercise of its constitutional powers."[36]

Factors Influencing State Support for Refugees

How do states emphasize their needs in a way that does not conflict with the federal government? Not easily as the opening chapter vignette also illustrated. While refugee resettlement has been politicized recently and framed as something that takes away states' rights, it was not always that way. In fact, states were once a crucial and vocal supporter of refugee resettlement. We will look at several possible factors in this final section before transitioning to an examination of public opinion data and polling in Chapter 6.

One reason for the decline in state support for refugees was the perception that they were less economically independent and more in need of short- and long-term welfare and assistance to figure out their new lives in the United States. For example, support was quite high in the United States for the first wave of Cuban refugees, many wealthy, between 1959 and 1962 but deteriorated as Americans saw later cohorts of Cubans—1965 to 1964, 1980, 1993 to 1995—as being less educated with fewer educational and work experiences.[37] President Lyndon B. Johnson also made a public appeal to voluntary agencies for their support in assisting the new Cuban refugees with a particular emphasis on organizations in Florida where the Cuban diaspora was having the greatest impact.[38]

Another group that experienced a similar pattern of support followed by opposition were Southeast Asian refugees (then called Indochinese). While the first cohort of Vietnamese refugees in 1975 was accepted

35. Barry R.Weingast, and John Ferejohn. 1997. "States' Rights—and Wrongs." Hoover Digest (Hoover Institution), October 30. https://www.hoover.org/research/states-rights-and-wrongs

36. Stephanie Jurkowski. 2017. "Supremacy Clause." Legal Information Institute (Cornell University). https://www.law.cornell.edu/wex/supremacy_clause

37. PBS. 2005. "Cuban Exiles in America." An American Experience. https://www.pbs.org/wgbh/americanexperience/features/castro-cuban-exiles-america/

38. Susan F. Martin. 2021. A Nation of Immigrants, 2nd ed. New York: Cambridge University Press, p. 233.

warmly—although there was some resistance, particularly in Texas[39]—the same could not be said for the Cambodian and Hmong refugees who arrived in the United States in the late 70s and early 80s. These later arrivals had:

> far fewer personal and financial resources than the 1975 refugees … Many of the Cambodians had no more than a few years of education, if any. A disproportionately large number of households headed by women were resettled, the men not having survived the Khmer Rouge years. The Hmong from Laos came from a society that had no written alphabet until one was created for them in the 1950s. The vast majority of the Hmong who entered the United States were illiterate.[40]

States rarely act alone, often adapting policies and borrowing legislation from other states, particularly those in proximity geographically and ideologically (a process known as policy diffusion).[41] This has been well documented among states with less professional legislatures, i.e., part-time legislators, who often meet only for a very short legislative session, maintain their professional careers outside state politics, and have minimal staffs. Scholars have determined that states with more professional legislatures may borrow policy ideas from other states but will reinvent or change bills' language; what they term "copy and paste lawmaking."[42]

The American Legislative Exchange Council (ALEC) has been described as a "super interest group" that goes well beyond helping states craft conservative legislation; state legislators paid them, for example, to write bills on Stand Your Ground policies with strikingly similar language across states.[43] ALEC has also been associated with diffusion and writing legislation opposing sanctuary policy[44] and state pre-emption of public health and emergency powers.[45]

In 2016, Tennessee legislators introduced "six bills that sought to create barriers for refugee resettlement." While none made it out of committee to a vote, the most extreme bill "attempted to create a refugee registry that would hold sponsors civilly liable for any violent crimes or terrorist-related acts committed by the sponsored refugee." In a case of policy diffusion, South Carolina legislators attempted their own refugee-policy coup following Tennessee's lead but without gubernatorial support. They introduced a resolution permitting "the state's attorney

39. Agnes Constante. 2020. "Documentary Looks at 1970s Racial Tension Between Vietnamese, Whites in Texas Town." NBC News, May 4. https://www.nbcnews.com/news/asian-america/documentary-looks-1970s-racial-tension-between-vietnamese-whites-texas-town-n1199846

40. Susan F. Martin. 2021. A Nation of Immigrants, 2nd ed. New York: Cambridge University Press, p. 237.

41. Stefano DellaVigna, and Woojin Kim. 2022. "Policy Diffusion and Polarization Across U.S. States." National Bureau of Economic Research, June. https://www.nber.org/papers/w30142

42. Joshua M. Jansa, Eric R. Hansen, and Virginia H. Gray. 2018. "Copy and Paste Lawmaking: Legislative Professionalism and Policy Reinvention in the States." American Politics Research, 47 (4): 739–767.

43. Stephanie L. DeMora, Loren Collingwood, and Adriana Ninci. 2019. "The Role of Super Interest Groups in Public Policy Diffusion." Policy & Politics, 47 (4): 513–541.

44. Loren Collingwood, Stephen Omar El-Khatib, and Benjamin Gonzalez O'Brien. 2019. "Sustained organizational influence: American Legislative Exchange Council and the diffusion of anti-sanctuary policy." Policy Studies Journal 47 (3): 735–773.

45. Elizabeth Platt, Katie Moran-McCabe, Amy Cook, and Scott Burris. 2023. "Trends in U.S. State Public Health Emergency Laws, 2021–2022." American Journal of Public Health 113 (3): 288–296.

general to commence legal action against the federal government if it had failed to consult with the state about planned resettlements within its borders." The resolution did not pass.[46]

Another prime example of policy diffusion, not related to immigration specifically but tangentially, has been the authorship, sponsorship, and partisanship associated with bills to "curb" Muslim influence in the United States through anti-sharia[47] law measures. Shaykh Faraz Rabbani, an American Muslim religious scholar, says that the Arabic phrase, "Shariah, means the clear, well-trodden path to water. Islamically, it is used to refer to the matters of religion that God has legislated for His servants."[48] According to Dr. Daniel Hummel, a political scientist, the 2010 Ground Zero mosque controversy was the kindling that became the fire, which was eventually also reignited by President Trump's rhetoric. Subsequently, "It is not a coincidence that in 2010 the first batch of anti-Sharia laws reached state legislatures."[49] Twelve states would eventually adopt anti-Sharia laws between 2010 and 2019—Alabama, Arizona, Arkansas, Florida, Kansas, Louisiana, Mississippi, North Carolina, Oklahoma, Tennessee, Texas, and South Dakota.[50]

List of Key Takeaways

- One of President Donald Trump's most contentious policies was Executive Order 13888, which allowed cities and state governments to refuse the resettlement of refugees if the local or state officials were not consulted and did not approve the plans.
- The policy was eventually blocked in court but generated a flurry of debate about the role of states in refugee resettlement and about federalism broadly.
- It also reignited interest in the states' rights doctrine, which emphasizes that states are more representative of American citizens' needs than the federal government.
- Although there are many countries in the world that operate under federalism, it is uniquely different in the United States because states are allowed to create their own policies if there is no federal mandate or jurisdiction.
- If the Constitution does not specify what is a congressional power, then those powers or policy areas are given to the states (according to the Ninth and Tenth Amendments).
- Another feature that is confusing is how many federal programs, like SNAP, are administered by states. This means that benefits may vary by state.
- Historically, the federal government has operated its Refugee Admissions Program (RAP) by working with

46. Patrick Benjamin. 2021. "State Refugee Policies: A Reflection on National Discourses on Immigration." In Immigration, Key to the Future: The Benefits of Resettlement to Upstate New York. Albany: New York State Bar Association, 101–110, p. 107.

47. Also spelled Sharia, shariah, and Shariah.

48. Faraz Rabbani. 2011. "What Is the Shariah? A Path to God, a Path to Good." Seekers Guidance, March 8. https://seekersguidance.org/articles/general-artices/what-is-the-shariah-a-path-to-god-a-path-to-good-faraz-rabbani/

49. Daniel Hummel. 2021. Prejudice and Policymaking: Islamophobia in the United States and the Diffusion of Anti-Sharia Laws. London: Lexington Books, p. 8.

50. Ibid, p. 12

private refugee resettlement organizations (RROs), which then allocate funding and resources to local affiliates in cities and towns to specifically help groups of refugees.

- Although 49 states resettle refugees, they do have discretion as to how those programs are managed. Some states are very involved in the resettlement process while others partner with private agencies (and in a few states, the whole program is administered by private, nongovernmental organizations).

- Thirteen states also utilize a special structure known as the Wilson-Fish Program where Office of Refugee Resettlement (ORR) funding is given directly to one agency in each state which is then responsible for administering the resources. This is supposed to be more efficient than ORR funding multiple agencies and offices in each state, and some research supports this assertion.

- Several factors influence why and how states support refugees. One is the perception that some refugees are more economically beneficial to some states than others.

- Another factor is how states view other states' policies. If there is support for what another government does, a state may borrow the components and language of another state and pass its own legislation. This is called policy diffusion.

- For example, Tennessee tried to limit resettlement in 2016 through the introduction of several bills. Although none passed, South Carolina made its own failing attempts to restrict refugee policies.

Chapter Review Questions

1. **Which** of the following features of SNAP make its implementation so confusing?
   a. It is funded completely by state taxes but implemented at the federal level.
   b. It is only available to immigrants and refugees.
   c. It is a federal policy implemented by states, which have some discretion about the amount of assistance people receive. (CORRECT)
   d. It only benefits Americans in richer states like California.

2. **Show** ONE example of how political culture influenced a state's response to COVID.

3. **Define** "replacement designee."

4. **Summarize** your understanding of the five steps of refugee admissions and resettlement.
   A.
   B.
   C.
   D.
   E.

5. **Explain** why American perception of Cubans changed between the 1950s and 1990s.

6. According to Dr. Daniel Hummel, what event triggered a national debate on sharia law in the United States?
   a. President Barack Obama's inauguration.
   b. The planned construction of a mosque near Ground Zero. (CORRECT)
   c. President Trump's 2020 election loss.
   d. The recent presence of more Afghan interpreters and soldiers in the United States.

Critical Thinking Questions

1. **Explain** the relationship between the professionalism of a state legislature and the likelihood of it engaging in policy diffusion. Why should it matter?
2. Imagine you are an advisor to one of the 2024 presidential candidates. Can you **formulate** a policy that protects the interests of states and the primary of the national government when it comes to refugee resettlement? Or is the loss of state power a foregone conclusion?
3. **Assess** this statement from the chapter: "Federalism shapes the lives of every American citizen, resident, and even tourist whether they want to believe it or not." Provide ONE example of a policy—not mentioned in this chapter—that illustrates this quote.

CHAPTER 6

American Support for Refugees

Opening Vignette

The video starts with one man: "My name's Chris Buckley. I'm a former U.S. Army sergeant, recovering drug addict, former KKK Imperial Nighthawk." It transitions to another: "My name is Heval Kelli, and my story is like the story of any refugee in the world." ABC News's Michael Koenig then asks Kelli, "Why would you befriend a member of the KKK?" Heval shrugs his shoulders and replies, "Why not?" So begins a remarkable 2019 interview[1] highlighting a relationship between a white man from Georgia who was raised to hate others, and a brown Kurdish Muslim refugee who was taught to love. At one point in the interview, Buckley tells Koenig that he felt an "immediate, just connection" with Dr. Kelli, especially after hearing about this journey. According to Buckley, "We start talking and he tells me a story, and it's like, 'Wow. You're a refugee from Syria, came 10 days after 9/11. You worked your way into med school, washing dishes and drilling yourself on vocabulary.' I kind of felt unjustified by hatred, you know?"

Figure 6.1   Dr. Heval Kelli rests his hand on the shoulder of his friend, Chris Buckley.

1. Localish. 2019. "Former KKK Member & Syrian Muslim Refugee Form Inspiring Friendship." More in Common. https://www.youtube.com/watch?v=4XqbH5Iu3lo

Buckley and Kelli's friendship is the basis for the 2022 documentary *REFUGE*,[2] which explores each of their paths to an initial meeting that would change their lives. Subtitled "A Story About Fear and Love in the American South," the film's website cogently states three objectives with the expectation "that after watching *REFUGE*, viewers will have an awakened sense of empathy." Accordingly, "Our impact and education campaign has three goals—to advocate for refugees, to prevent radicalization, and to build empathy across race, faith, and political ideology."[3]

QR Code 6.1

Introduction to the Chapter

The opening vignette showcased a stellar example of what psychologist Robert Zajonc termed "mere exposure" in 1968. According to the then-novel hypothesis, "mere repeated exposure of the individual to a stimulus is a sufficient condition for the enhancement of his attitude toward it."[4] Chris Buckley was exposed to Dr. Heval Kelli, a Muslim refugee, and this stimulus enhanced and transformed Buckley's attitudes Toward not only Kelli but Muslims broadly. Research has also shown how effective exposure can be to wanting fewer restrictions for immigrants,[5] reducing transphobia,[6] and increasing support for Latinos (particularly having Latinx friends).[7] This last exposure phenomenon is also known by what psychologist Thomas Pettigrew called "the friendship potential"—"real opportunities for immigrants and natives to become friends and that typically requires interactions across times and different social contexts."[8]

2. https://www.refugemovie.com/

3. https://www.refugemovie.com/impact

4. Robert B. Zajonc. 1968. "Attitudinal Effects of Mere Exposure." *Journal of Personality and Social Psychology* 9 (2): 1–27.

5. Kathleen M. Moore. 2002. "'United We Stand': American Attitudes Toward (Muslim) Immigration Post-September 11th." The Muslim World, 92: 39–57.

6. David Broockman, and Joshua Kalla. 2016. "Durably Reducing Transphobia: A Field Experiment on Door-to-Door Canvassing." *Science*, 352 (6282): 220–224. https://www.science.org/doi/10.1126/science.aad9713

7. Christopher G. Ellison, Heeju Shin, and David L. Leal. 2011. "The Contact Hypothesis and Attitudes Toward Latinos in the United States." *Social Science Quarterly* 92(4): 938–58.

8. Frank Tao. 2020. "What Research Says About the Effects of Contact With Immigrants." Social Science Research Methods Center (Study of Studies), November 12. https://ssrmc.wm.edu/what-research-says-about-the-effects-of-contact-with-immigrants/

Political socialization is the study of how people become political; the "research strives to understand where citizens' political views and actions come from and what causes them to change."[9] The pioneering work in this area examined how much influence parents have on the political attitudes of their children, particularly "preadults" (teenagers now).[10] Research also looked at the earliest memories of children, even as toddlers, and what they potentially imbibe from their parents. According to child psychiatrist Robert Coles,

> As soon as we are born, in most places on this earth, we acquire a nationality, a membership in a community … The infant knows nothing of this event, but the parents certainly are aware of it, and what they know or feel as citizens, as subjects, as comrades, is communicated to the child in the first years of life.[11]

Another influential scholar, psychologist Gordon Allport, suggested that "as early as the age of five, a child is capable of understanding that he is a member of various groups. He is capable, for example, of a sense of ethnic identification." Allport goes on to write that even if the child does not understand specific ethnic labels, he still "develops fierce in-group loyalties."[12]

Unfortunately, the reality is that most people do not have the opportunity to meet or befriend refugees, and this lack of exposure directly influences how the former responds to the latter. That does not necessarily mean that people have to get to know refugees to develop positive, encouraging, and warm feelings that translate into acceptance. But there is no question that the very idea of a refugee, or immigrant broadly, triggers differential responses in people based on their own backgrounds, ideologies, previous experiences with immigration, and other factors. That is the focus of this chapter. We will first explore what research has shown about attitudes toward immigrants and refugees and then look specifically at public opinion polling data toward refugees from the 1930s to the present day.

The Question: Where do you get your information about refugees? What influences your opinion about refugees coming to this country?

Learning Objectives

Reading this chapter will enable readers to:

- **Summarize** an understanding of the key terms related to public opinion polling.
- **Interpret** polling toward refugees and glean new insights.
- **Explore** the variables affecting how Americans perceive refugees.
- **Propose** solutions to improving support for refugees.

9. Laura Stoker, and Jackie Bass. 2011. "Political Socialization: Ongoing Questions and New Directions." In The Oxford Handbook of American Public Opinion and the Media, ed. George C. Edwards, Lawrence R. Jacobs, and Robert Y. Shapiro. New York: Oxford University Press, 453–470, p. 460.

10. Kent M. Jennings, and Richard G. Niemi. 1968. "The Transmission of Political Values from Parent to Child." *American Political Science Review* 62 (1): 169–184.

11. Robert Coles. 1986. The Political Life of Children. Boston: *Atlantic Monthly Press*, p. 59–60.

12. Gordon W. Allport. 1979 (1954). The Nature of Prejudice (Unabridged). Boston: Addison-Wesley, p. 29.

What Is Polling, and What Can It Teach Us?

Political science, like many disciplines, is largely empirical, which means that conclusions about how people think are derived from individual and group observations. Let's say, for example, you wanted to know how Alabama residents rated the performance of Senator Katie Britt, the first woman to represent the state in the U.S. Senate, after her rebuttal of the 2024 State of the Union. The population could be all residents of Alabama, but a better one might be all registered voters in the state, or even all registered voters who cast a ballot for Britt in 2022. Since it is impossible to gather the opinions of every single person in a population like the ones mentioned above, we need to randomly select a smaller group of people who represent the population and do it in such a way that every person in that sample had the same probability of being chosen (also known as a random sample). Each participant in a poll is one data point, and a collection of these data points makes up the sample used by researchers to estimate the political views of a certain population being studied.

Public opinion polling on refugees follows the principles laid about above. For more clarity, let us look at a 2020 APM survey on refugee resettlement. The population is unspecified, but we can deduce it is either all Americans or all Americans over the age of 18. The poll was conducted between December 10 and 15, 2020, over the phone through random-digit dialing (RDD) of landlines and cellphones. The sample was 1,003 respondents with almost all participating in English (only 35 in Spanish).[13] Participants were asked the following:

> Now thinking specifically about refugees; that is, those who have fled their home country due to persecution or conflict and were allowed to settle in the U.S. Do you think decisions on where refugees should be resettled should be primarily left up to the federal government, state governments, or local governments?

The results indicate that 38% of respondents believe decisions should be left to the federal government; 25% with state governments; 23% with local governments; 8% say a mix of governments; and 7% did not know or refused to answer. It is important to note the presence of a margin of error, which is common in public opinion polling. This tells us the range of possible values when understanding a sample's perspective on a certain question. So, the actual percentage who believe the federal government should be in charge of resettlement based on APM's 3.5% margin of error is a range of values from 34.5% to 41.5%. This matters because even with an additional 3.5%, there are still more respondents who favor the federal government over the state government.[14]

The biggest challenge to truly understanding how Americans feel about refugees is the lack of continuous longitudinal data on the topic (Figure 6.2). Public opinion polling on refugees is reactive; polls are commissioned only in response to certain crises and are often not yearly, which leads to huge gaps in data. There are many organizations and news sites that conduct national polls—Monmouth University's Polling Institute, Pew Research

---

13. https://static1.squarespace.com/static/5c9542c8840b163998cf4804/t/5e334a8d74383164f98b8fe5/1580419726055/immigration-survey-transparency-disclosure-and-methods-january-2020.pdf

14. APM Survey. 2020. "What Do Americans Think About Refugee Resettlement?" APM Research Lab, February 21. https://static1.squarespace.com/static/5c9542c8840b163998cf4804/t/5e4ee59b5696825742186f6c/1582228892399/apm-survey-Feb-2020-refugee-resettlement-FINAL.pdf

Center, CBS, Roper, Gallup, *New York Times*, Public Religion Research Institute (PRRI), National Opinion Research Center (NORC), Harris, and the Quinnipiac University Polling Institute. But these organizations will only conduct polls based on a need for data about the political crises of the time. We should note that the federal government recently started surveying refugees themselves to learn more about their needs (before and after arrival), integration challenges, and access to healthcare.[15]

Poll Question: "How serious a problem do you think the issue of illegal immigration is for the United States right now – very, somewhat, not too, or not at all serious?

	September 2015	September 2017	January 2018	November 2018
Very serious	45%	43%	45%	49%
Somewhat serious	30%	30%	25%	21%
Not too serious	15%	17%	16%	15%
Not at all serious	9%	10%	13%	13%
Don't know	2%	1%	1%	1%
Sample size (n)	1,009	1,009	806	802

Figure 6.2   Attitudes Toward Illegal Immigration.

Data Source: https://www.monmouth.edu/polling-institute/reports/monmouthpoll_us_111918/

Figure 6.2 is an example of immigration-related polling done right, which avoids the problem above about insufficient longitudinal data. Between November 9 and 12, 2018, the Polling Institute at Monmouth University in West Long Branch, New Jersey, conducted a national survey of 1,009 adults to gauge attitudes on illegal immigration.[16] This was the fourth wave of the survey; previous polls were conducted in September 2015, September 2017, January 2018, and then November 2018. This is a well-conducted survey that provides political scientists with four, time-related data points, which then allows us to compare public opinion over time (as continuous longitudinal data).

Polling is also often related to perceptions of certain groups based on preexisting (implicit) religious, racial, ethnic, and political biases. So, it is difficult, if not impossible, to parse out how Americans feel about certain minorities versus how these groups might be viewed as refugees first (and as minorities second). How a survey question is phrased has a huge impact on how the question is received by a respondent. Altering the language, including nouns and verbs, an interviewer's accent, and even tone can all affect different responses. Survey questions can also lead respondents to specific types of answers; these are aptly called leading questions. Recent work by sociologist Dr. Mariano Sana also points to survey respondents more likely to be sympathetic toward refugees when

15. Nicol Valdez. 2021. "Introducing the New Annual Survey of Refugees (ASR)." Office of Planning, Research, and Evaluation, Administration for Children & Families (US Department of Health and Human Services), March 9. https://www.acf.hhs.gov/opre/blog/2021/03/introducing-new-annual-survey-refugees-asr-2020

16. Monmouth University. 2018. "Public Divided on Whether Migrant Caravan Poses a Threat." Monmouth University Polling Institute (Monmouth Poll Reports), November 19. https://www.monmouth.edu/polling-institute/reports/monmouthpoll_us_111918/

asked about refugees who have already arrived in the United States and "an increase in support for refugee admissions when questions provide context *and* refer to real-world scenarios or policies involving refugees."[17]

Roper's 1938 poll asked Americans if they supported bringing in "German, Austrian, and other political refugees." This is a poor question because it asks the participant to offer support about three groupings of people; the survey participant must combine their thoughts about Germans, Austrians, and "other political refugees," which implies that the first two groups are also fleeing political persecution. In 1955, the National Opinion Research Center (NORC) asked Americans about their support for European refugees, but in the 1957 poll, asked about people who had lost their homes to "Communists." This will likely trigger a completely different survey response because it hooks into how an American might feel about Communism, which might artificially bump the level of support for Europeans, who are now also victims of Communist violence.

Figure 6.3   Pro-refugee protestors in 2017.

17. Mariano Sana. 2021. "Public Opinion on Refugee Policy in the United States, 1938–2019: Increasing Support for Refugees and the Sympathy
Effect." International Migration Review, 55 (2): 574–604, p. 576.

Similarly, a 2002 Hamilton College poll asked a sample of Americans their thoughts on accepting refugees from Iraq but included a question on those "fleeing from Saddam Hussein." Like the other questions mentioned above, this statement changes how the respondent now might think about refugees from Iraq based on how they feel about Saddam Hussein. If they are already opposed to Hussein, then this will increase the likelihood of support for Iraqi refugees (and at least more than they might have said without a reference to the dictator). Lastly, multiple polls in 2015 and 2016 asked respondents about their support for Syrians *and* Muslims. This is also a poor question because a respondent is now being asked about religion. The refugees are not just Syrian but also now Muslim, which might trigger an implicit Islamophobic bias that depresses support for Syrian refugees because the survey participant does not like Muslims.

The other considerable challenge is the type of question and question wording. For example, the Roper Center's iPOLL database contains 698 refugee-related survey questions asked of Americans between 1938 and 2023. Many of these questions, however, are loosely related to refugees. These include questions about attitudes toward refugees in camps; attitudes about presidents handling refugee crises; retrospective calculations about number of past refugees; giving military permission to protect refugees; refugees and terrorism; if the U.S. has a moral obligation to take in a set number of refugees; attitudes toward the U.N. or UNHCR; and opinions on whether unaccompanied minors should be treated as refugees. These are all important social science questions, but none of the above specifically get to how an American might feel about the United States offering asylum to refugees.

What Shapes Public Opinion Toward Refugees?

In 1972, American economist Anthony Downs contrived a theory to explain why American public opinion on the environment had shifted so quickly from a topic of little interest to suddenly something everyone cared about. "Each of these problems," wrote Downs, "suddenly leaps into prominence, remains there for a short time, and then—though still largely unresolved—gradually fades from the center of public attention."[18] How did important topics that seemingly had the full attention of the public disappear just as quickly?

Downs's "issue-attention cycle" elegantly connected public opinion, policymaking, and response to political stimuli. The five stages of his cycle start with a "preproblem stage" (a problem exists, but not enough people know about it yet); "alarmed discovery and euphoric enthusiasm" (any problem can be fixed with enough determination, allegedly); "realizing the cost of significant progress"; "gradual decline of intense public interest"; and "the postproblem stage."[19] Downs accurately predicted the final stage as one where "an issue that has been replaced at the center of public concern moves into a prolonged limbo—a twilight realm of less attention or spasmodic recurrences of interest."[20]

While Downs's cycle continues to be celebrated half a century later, there are also criticisms of its simplicity. Why is the government's response to a political crisis not featured in stage three? Does any policymaking occur

18. Anthony Downs. 1972. "Up and Down with Ecology: The 'Issue-Attention Cycle.'" *The Public*, 38–50, p. 38.
19. Ibid, p. 39–40.
20. Ibid, p. 40.

before the public realizes the "cost of significant progress," and how are costs measured?[21] Where is the influence of "information and/or misinformation … in reshaping an issue during the euphoric enthusiasm stage"? And what happens when "extreme points of view" cast aside "workable, practical policy solutions and created inertia"?[22]

Public reaction to refugees is one of the policy arenas that meets many of the criteria of the issue-attention cycle, despite its limitations, because it gets at the heart of many of the political debates in the United States. As we already discussed in other chapters, attitudes toward refugees are an even more nuanced type of political feeling than thoughts about immigrants broadly because of the singular nature of why refugees are people of displacement in need of urgent humanitarian assistance. Since the United States "describes itself as 'a country of immigrants,'" according to a pair of researchers, "it has made the absorption of immigrants a basic and distinctive characteristic of its heritage."[23]

Yet, they also note that "the one major and consistent theme that is sharply and clearly defined in each country's responses to national public opinion polls is that in no country … does a majority of citizens have positive feelings about their current cohort of immigrants." The American pattern is "the tendency to look at immigrants with rose-colored glasses turned backwards."[24] The public and elites are constantly torn about the need to present the United States as welcoming. We/they are insistent that a certain way of life must be maintained at all costs even if keeping up appearances means not welcoming everyone: "One legend puts the immigrant, and all he represents, at the center of American experience. Another relegates him to the periphery."[25]

Multiple theories abound as to the source of anti-immigrant rhetoric and hysteria and how those behaviors affect public support. Public opinion about refugees is often affected by perceptions about some being "difficult to assimilate" and poorly skilled when it comes to joining and improving the job market.[26] These "economic anxieties" then act as a vehicle for pre-existing prejudices about immigrants.[27]

21. Guy B. Peters, and Brian W. Hogwood. 1985. "In Search of the Issue-Attention Cycle." *Journal of Politics*, 47 (1): 238–253, p. 239.

22. Maria A. Reyes. 2010. "Immigration Attention Cycle." Public Administration Review (Book Review), 70 (6): 957960, p. 958.

23. Rita J. Simon, and James P. Lynch. 1999. "A Comparative Assessment of Public Opinion Toward Immigrants and Immigration Policies." The International Migration Review, 33 (2): 455–467, p. 455.

24. Ibid, p. 458.

25. John Higham. 1993 (1975). Send These to Me: Immigrants in Urban America. Baltimore: The Johns Hopkins University Press, p. 4.

26. Rawan Arar, and David Scott Fitzgerald. 2023. The Refugee System: A Sociological Approach. Cambridge, UK: Polity Press, p. 244.

27. Peter Burns, and James G. Gimpel. 2000. "Economic Insecurity, Prejudicial Stereotypes, and Public Opinion on Immigration Policy." *Political Science Quarterly* 115 (2): 201–225.

Support for Refugees

- I looked at 102 polls between 1938 and 2022, a span of 84 years.
- Each poll asked respondents if they supported or opposed accepting refugees broadly or specific groups of refugees based on country, religion, and other factors.
- The mean level of support was 42.63% and mean level of opposition was 51.88%.
- On average, across all years and data points, opposition to refugees coming to the United States exceeded support.
- The only exception was the national response to Ukrainian refugees in 2022, which Gallup noted was the highest ever recorded since they began polling on the topic.[28]

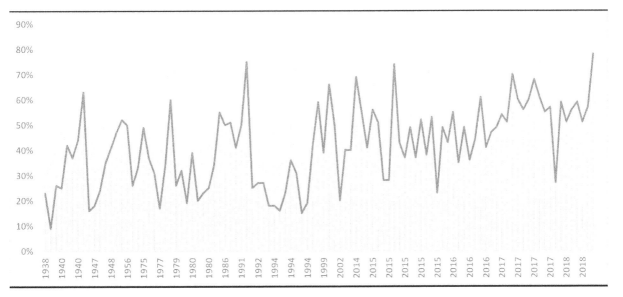

Figure 6.4   Public Opinion Support for Refugees Over Time.

It is also challenging to isolate public approval from the broader criteria that affect how everyday people feel or are taught to feel about political figures and events. Media coverage, rhetoric and speeches from politicians, and individual backgrounds and biographies may all shape how we think. An American citizen, for instance, whose family recently emigrated to the United States, and who still has cousins and grandparents in the country of origin, will have a very different opinion about someone who is seeking asylum now in the U.S. versus an American whose family was displaced due to the First World War and has lived here for over a century.

28. Lydia Saad. 2022. "Americans Widely Favor Welcoming Ukrainian Refugees." Gallup, April 2. https://news.gallup.com/poll/392069/americans-widely-favor-welcoming-ukrainian-refugees.aspx

Partisanship and political ideology can also make a massive impact on voters. A January 2024 Verasight Poll assessed American attitudes toward a multitude of political issues, including December 2023 comments by former President Donald Trump (which we discussed in Chapter 3). Not only was there sizable support for Trump's statements that immigrants "are destroying the blood of the country," but the more favorable people felt toward the Republican Party, the more likely they were to embrace this form of nativism. The opposite was true for participants who had more affinity toward the Democratic Party. Respondents who also voted for Trump in 2020 were significantly more likely to believe that immigration was deleterious to the country.[29]

Recency can also greatly mold how someone feels about a political issue, especially if the event was not previously salient. Let us look at a concrete example of this from an analysis of American public opinion toward Muslims after 9/11 in the context of trends toward immigrants. Dr. Kathleen Moore, a religious studies scholar, fielded a national sample just a month after the terrorist attacks. As expected, over half of respondents thought "Arab or Muslim immigration" should be decreased, around 39% felt it should stay at its current level, and only 2% said it should be increased.[30] Dr. Moore also asked people in the sample whether the number of Afghani immigrants should be maintained, increased, or lowered: "more than six in ten respondents (63%) support reducing or stopping Afghani immigration altogether."[31]

Similarly, after the November 2015 terrorist attacks in Paris (discussed in Chapter 1) and the December 2015 terrorist incident in San Bernardino, California, public opinion toward Muslims was generally low. And yet, Quinnipiac University still conducted a poll in December that included this question: "Which do you think poses a greater terrorist threat to the U.S.: terrorists hiding among Syrian refugees, radicalized foreign visitors, or so-called 'homegrown jihadists'?" A December 2015 CBS/NYT survey asked, "Which comes closer to your opinion about Syrian refugees who want to come to the United States?" The options were:

1. "The U.S. should allow refugees from Syria into the United States as long as they go through a security clearance process."
2. "The U.S. should not allow any refugees from Syria into the United States at this time."

Since several of these survey questions were fielded days after the December 2, 2015, San Bernardino, Calif., terrorist attack, the questions are focused on terrorism. A November 2015 CBS News Poll asked, "Do you think it is necessary for Syrian refugees who want to come to the United States to go through a stricter security clearance process than they do now or don't you think that is necessary?" Another pre-Paris question came from a November 2015 ABC/Washington Post poll: "How confident are you that the United States can identify and keep out possible terrorists who may be among these refugees (from the conflict in Syria and other Mideast countries)—very confident,

29. Shyam K. Sriram. 2024. "New Data Shows Many Americans Share Donald Trump's Anti-Immigration Views." United States Politics and Policy Blog (London School of Economics), February 13. https://blogs.lse.ac.uk/usappblog/2024/02/13/new-data-shows-many-americans-share-donald-trumps-anti-immigration-views/.
30. Kathleen M. Moore. 2002. "'United We Stand': American Attitudes toward (Muslim) Immigration Post-September 11th." The Muslim World, 92: 39–57, p. 44.
31. Ibid, p. 48.

somewhat confident, not so confident, or not confident at all?" These are not only examples of poor polling questions because of how muddled and biased the responses might be due to the conflation of terrorism with refugees and Islam, but the options for respondents are not clearly differentiated from each other.

Challenges to Building Support for Refugees

Despite everything you have read in this textbook about the desperation faced by refugees seeking some degree of normalcy compared to the chaos of displacement, the truth of our current time is that many people still find it hard to see refugees as people deserving *more* help. The challenge is getting a group of people to reach out across cultures, "convincing others to accept those across great social boundaries will always be an uphill slog."[32] Here are a few possible solutions to ameliorate support for refugees.

a) Providing Incentives to Care

The haves helping the have-nots requires more than exposure, more than an interest, and possibly even more than humanitarianism. It might require an incentive, what famed economist Dr. Mancur Olson regarded as the problem of collective action. According to a eulogy after Olson's death in 1998, "Joining groups is rational, not instinctive; forming groups is hard, not easy; and keeping groups together is problematic." Leaders gain participation from people/communities/teams when the benefits exceed the costs of doing so and when participants are offered a reward.[33]

One possible incentive is building support around accepting refugees who were also our allies in military operations. These include members of the Hmong (whom we discussed at the beginning of Chapter 4), Iraqi, and Afghani communities. This could tie into Olson's idea of a purposive incentive; in this case it would be patriotism and supporting the government and military. Polling has indicated a huge level of support among Americans for these refugees (66% of Americans in an August 2023 poll).[34] President Biden formalized the government's support of Afghani allies with Operation Allies Welcome (OAW), which was implemented by the secretary of defense and strongly supported by the military. Eight sites were established nationally as installations and safe havens, which ultimately supported and houses approximately 73,000 Afghani military allies, veterans, and their families.[35] The White House even created a list of ways that Americans could help Afghani allies, including donating air miles to families to travel and offering housing and job opportunities.[36]

32. Rawan Arar and David Scott Fitzgerald. 2023. The Refugee System: A Sociological Approach. Cambridge, UK: Polity Press, p. 245.

33. David Brooks. 1998. "Mancur Olson's Legacy." *The Washington Examiner* (The Weekly Standard), March 16. https://www.washingtonexaminer.com/weekly-standard/mancur-olsons-legacy

34. Dan Gordon. 2023. "New Survey: Americans Strongly Support Certainty for Afghan Allies." National Immigration Forum, August 14. https://immigrationforum.org/article/new-survey-americans-strongly-support-certainty-for-afghan-allies/

35. US Northern Command. 2022. "DoD Support to Operation Allies Welcome." https://www.northcom.mil/OAW/

36. Jack Markell and Nazanin Ash. 2021. "6 Ways to Welcome Our Afghan Allies." The White House (Briefing Room Blog), December 17. https://www.whitehouse.gov/briefing-room/blog/2021/12/17/6-ways-to-welcome-our-afghan-allies/

People will be more likely to help refugees when doing so benefits host societies more than we have previously discussed in this textbook. Two scholars recently argued that "Many of the most successful instances of refugee protection include an element of self-interest on the part of host states."[37] However, they candidly posit that most members of host societies have little understanding of the precarity surrounding politics and global disorder and how quickly an otherwise stable government might dissolve due to internal or external factors. This led the authors to surmise, "Today's hosts can become tomorrow's refugees."[38] One example of this paradox is Iraq, which has 1.2 million internally displaced people and provides asylum for over a quarter of a million refugees.[39]

b) Refugees as a Threat to Nationhood

It is well established by scholars that most Americans think that new immigrants, regardless of their reason to leave countries of origin or motivation to arrive in the United States, represent a challenge or threat to what it means to be American (even though all Americans, with the exception of the indigenous, were also immigrants or their descendants at one time). But what really makes some Americans see immigration as a threat is when identity, particularly white identity, becomes the pathway "through which Americans are filtering their immigration attitudes."[40]

The argument is that white Americans see increased immigration as a concurrent loss of status; "population changes as a result of immigration threatens to displace whites numerically, and immigrants challenge the notion of America as a prototypically white nation."[41] Recent research has also pointed to the startling realization that non-white Americans can also become "new nativist publics," who are primed to oppose immigration because these minorities have internalized a sense of white normativity, too.[42] The problem with this form of thinking, however, is that it is predicated on the myth that Americans of European descent had a common background when, in fact, they spoke different languages, adhered to conflicted Christian customs, and only became white over time.[43]

c) The Diversity Binary

In *Still a House Divided*, political scientists Rogers Smith and Desmond King articulated a simple but powerful formula to explain the almost invincible nature of racial politics. America is constantly at war with itself, they argued, due to two fundamentally distinct ways of being. One group recognizes the primacy of race in every aspect of American political life and demands "race conscious" public policy (often pursued as multiculturalism). The other

37. Arar and Fitzgerald. 2023. 245.

38. Ibid, p. 248.

39. UNHCR. 2023. "Iraq Refugee Crisis." https://www.unrefugees.org/emergencies/iraq/

40. Ashley Jardina. 2019. White Identity Politics. Cambridge, UK: Cambridge University Press. p. 167.

41. Ibid, p. 185.

42. Shyam K. Sriram, Chloe McCarthy, and Analee DeGlopper. "Nativism and Islamophobia Might Explain Why Some Asian Pacific Americans Have Anti-Refugee Attitudes." U.S. Politics and Policy Blog, London School of Economics, July 28.

43. John S. W. Park. 2018. Immigration Law and Society. Cambridge, UK: Polity Press, p. 12.

group recognizes the past primacy of race but sees American political development as "postracial," which stipulates, in their minds, the need for "colorblind" public policy.[44]

Perhaps the inability of Americans to reach any consensus on immigration policy is also due to a binary conflict of another kind: "diversity" versus "homogeneity."[45] Refugees are deeply affected by this racial project in three ways: constantly changing policy and definitions over who is allowed and denied entrance; confused implementation across local, state, and federal lines; and explicitly biased expectations and limited resources. At no point in the process of accepting political immigrants into the U.S., giving them the official designation as "refugees," welcoming them to one of the dozen resettlement sites, or helping with the initial readjustment phase are refugees even remotely aware that the United States government has not accepted them due to some overwhelmingly sense of American altruism. Rather, as refugees come to realize, living in America means abandoning personhood for nationhood and relying on a government that could, and still does, change its mind frequently about who belongs … and who does not.

We do want to end this chapter on a positive note. Immigrants and refugees make our country better, and recent polling confirms this. A Pew Research Center poll showed that 46% of Americans in 2016 believed that a newcomer "strengthens American society," which jumped to 60% in 2020. Conversely, the share of Americans who believed that a newcomer "threatens traditional American customs and values" dropped from 50% in 2016 to 37% in 2020.[46] These numbers are indicative of a national acceptance toward immigration, previously strong, that dropped during the Trump Presidency. Americans can be supportive of refugees specifically, but it will also be an uphill battle to convince at least some fellow citizens that immigration makes the country stronger and does not diminish our values.

List of Key Takeaways

- "Mere exposure" is a psychological theory developed by Robert Zajonc that advocates for individuals to experience or be exposed to a stimulus over and over, which will change a person's attitude toward something.
- This theory has been proven multiple times. Exposure to a conversation on trans rights diminishes transphobia and having Latinx friends improves attitudes toward Latinos.
- The opening vignette illustrated the theory's success in the friendship between a white supremacist and a Muslim refugee, who became close because repeated meetings opened their hearts and minds to accepting the other.

44. Desmond King, and Rogers M. Smith. 2011. Still a House Divided: Race and Politics in Obama's America. Princeton, NJ: Princeton University Press.

45. John Higham. 1993 (1975). Send These to Me: Immigrants in Urban America. Baltimore: The Johns Hopkins University Press, p. 4.

46. America's Voice. 2020. "Pew Poll on Immigrants and Refugees Finds Trump Has Forced Americans to Make a Choice—And We Have." September 11. https://americasvoice.org/press_releases/pew-poll-on-immigrants-and-refugees-finds-trump-has-forced-americans-to-make-a-choice-and-we-have/

- However, changing public opinion toward refugees can be challenging because most people do not have exposure or access to people from different backgrounds. This is also difficult because political beliefs start young in people, even as children.
- A key method of gauging political attitudes is through public opinion polls. These provide empirical data, which is obtained from individual and group behavior.
- The first step is choosing a population or a group of people that needs to be studied. Next, the researcher must randomly choose a smaller group from within that population, known as the sample, that represents the attitudes of the larger group.
- There is usually a certain amount of sample error that lets us know the range of possible values in public opinion. So, if 50% of a sample say they love mint chocolate chip ice cream, and the sample error is + 5, it means that the range of people who love that flavor is actually 45%–55%.
- The challenge with really understanding how Americans feel about refugees is that polls about refugees are not done yearly, and sometimes there might be a gap of several years between polls. We cannot know for certain how Americans feel about refugees yearly and if that support increases or decreases based on certain phenomena or beliefs.
- The other big problem is that every poll is asking Americans about different groups of people. One year it might be Hungarians and the next Iraqis.
- A macro examination of polling data between 1938 and 2022 showed that on average, Americans are more likely to be opposed to refugee resettlement than accepting people.
- Another drawback to figuring out refugee-related attitudes is that so many variables influence how an individual could feel about the topic.
- For example, are people opposed to Syrian refugees actually antirefugee or Islamophobic? If an individual has an irrational fear of Muslims—the definition of a phobia—then it probably will shape an opinion about refugees.
- Polling responses are also affected by the structure of a question; perception of an interviewer; and questions that lead people to choose certain answers.
- A 1955 poll asked Americans if they were open to accepting European refugees, but the language was changed two years later to ask if we should accept refugees whose homes were taken by Communists. This is a very different question that may lead to a completely different response.
- Recency, or the relative nearness of a poll to a major event, has a dramatic influence on people's answers.
- There are also cultural and environmental factors that influence public opinion. One problem in the United States is that public opinion sometimes seems to come out of nowhere on political issues and then disappear abruptly. Economist Anthony Downs predicted this with his 1972 "issue-attention cycle."
- While many Americans support immigration, there are others who feel that new immigrants are a burden to a society that already struggles with unemployment.
- One group also believes that immigration is a threat to national identity. This is especially true among Americans who identify as white and who see immigration as an attack on white cultural domination, which has been the historic norm.

- Still other Americans whose families are recent immigrants may be more supportive of immigration than someone whose family came on the Mayflower.
- One way of changing public opinion might be to offer an incentive to get people onboard. Supporting recent Afghani refugees or asylum seekers who served honorably with the American military could be a way to get patriotic Americans to develop more positive feelings toward refugees.

Chapter Review Questions

1. **Recall** the theory that best explains the friendship between Chris Buckley, the veteran turned Klansman, and Heval Kelli, the refugee turned doctor.
    a. The Hawthorne Effect
    b. The Issue-Attention Cycle
    c. Mere Exposure Theory (CORRECT)
    d. The Civic Voluntarism Model
2. **What** is the targeted population for a poll trying to measure the performance of U.S. Senator Katie Britt (R-Alabama)?
    a. Registered voters in Alabama. (CORRECT)
    b. High school students in Montgomery, Mobile, and Birmingham.
    c. Recently-admitted immigrants in Alabama.
    d. All of the above.
3. If 55% of respondents in a poll say the United States is not doing enough for refugees, and there is a sample error of + 6%, **what** can we learn from this information?
    a. Only 55% of the sample believe the United States is not doing enough for refugees.
    b. Only 6% of the sample think the United States is doing enough for refugees.
    c. 45% of the sample believe other countries should do more.
    d. The percentage of respondents who believe the United States is not doing enough ranges from 49% to 61%. (CORRECT)
4. **Which** of these is NOT a reason to explain opposition toward refugees?
    a. Americans are jealous of refugees and their large families. (CORRECT)
    b. Major events including terrorist attacks can lower support for refugees.
    c. Religious biases are often conflated with attitudes on immigration.
    d. Recent immigrants and their families may be less opposed toward refugees compared to people whose ancestry goes back decades or centuries.

5. **Rephrase** this quote: "These 'economic anxieties' then act as a vehicle for preexisting prejudices about immigrants."
    a. If someone already has a bias toward immigrants, that bias can worsen if triggered by thoughts that immigration is bad for the economy. (CORRECT)
    b. Immigrants only take jobs driving vehicles because they are out of sight, out of mind.
    c. "Economic anxieties" is just a way to cover the government's problem with people at the Canadian border.
    d. Immigrants often develop a dislike for natural-born Americans.
6. In two or three sentences, **summarize** the theory about how to get Americans to support recent Afghan evacuees more.
7. **Compare and contrast** the "race conscious" and "postracial" perspectives. Provide ONE example that shows how these two groups might see a policy differently.

Critical Thinking Questions

1. **Evaluate** Dr. Ashley Jardina's theory on identity politics. Do you agree with their argument that white identity is what motivates some Americans to oppose immigration?
2. Imagine that Gallup is fielding a national survey next year to gauge the opinions of Americans about asylum seekers from Malaysia seeking permanent residence in the United States. **Propose** ONE question for this survey that is an example of a good polling question *and* ONE example of a poor survey question. Compare and contrast them.
3. **What** are THREE conclusions about support for refugees from this figure? What do the polls tell us about public opinion over time? Can we compare and contrast the data?

CHAPTER 7

Current Challenges to Resettlement and Integration (with Cathryn Bennett)

Opening Vignette

On an especially cold morning in Guilford County, North Carolina, Cathryn and Rosie[1] met on one of Rosie's rare days off at her home in an affordable housing neighborhood, a 20-minute drive or 50-minute bus ride from the city center. With her three eldest children already enroute to school and her youngest contently yawning in her lap, Rosie's home was much quieter than usual for their visits in the evening for English practice. Despite the calm and coziness of the warmth inside, Rosie sighed heavily and looked askance at Cathryn before gently shaking her head and saying, "It's no good. I can't get to the school with the house and job and kids and husband." A few months prior, Rosie had begun work in a corrugated steel manufacturing plant on an early shift from 2 am–10 am; her employer provided transportation from her neighborhood to the plant about an hour away by car.

Rosie elaborated on her experience by stating, "… and the agency is gone; we have nobody. We are alone here[2]." Because Rosie and her family had been in the U.S. for four years at the time of this conversation, she was considered "outside" the time limit for agency support and services. In the first year, Rosie came to trust and rely on the many people she saw regularly: her caseworker, in particular, and a parade of volunteers the agency sent to her home had helped with understanding mail, applying for social services, and learning U.S. culture and communication. Now that Rosie and her husband were employed, the children were in school, and the family was beyond the first year, they did not see any of these people anymore.

Introduction to the Chapter

As we discussed earlier in Chapter 4, refugee integration during early resettlement, ranging from three to 12 months, is customarily addressed by agencies, typically federally funded responsible groups for refugees' transitions from places of temporary resettlement into the U.S. Community-based organizations (CBOs) that may or may not receive federal funding but which tend to operate with greater flexibility and humanization toward refugees are also important in the landscape of refugee resettlement vis-a-vis integration.

However, agencies are the first groups that convey legalistic aspects of refugee resettlement. Agencies typically approach integration through a one-size-fits-all mentality. While integration appears to prioritize matters of basic

---

1. Pseudonym used to protect identity.
2. Cathryn B. Bennett. 2022. "Refugee Women and Higher Education Across Space, Place, and Time." PhD Dissertation, University of North Carolina at Greensboro.

needs like language learning, cultural orientation, and employment, these aspects of integration are based on agency interpretation of a highly vague U.S. law pertaining to "self-sufficiency." As a result, self-sufficiency tends to be interpreted and applied as refugees obtaining jobs alone instead of the multiple diverse ways integration may be understood across cultures and backgrounds. The tension between aspirational and actual applications of self-sufficiency are elaborated on later in this chapter.

If Chapter 4 provided an overview of the structure and organization of resettlement, then this concluding chapter offers some real and negative examples of what happens when policies go badly for the displaced people these programs are supposed to help. Some of those failures include a pressure to assimilate, which may retraumatize refugees, and poor housing options that can cause more segregation. There is hope, however, and it takes the form of community-based organizations that fill in the gaps and provide key support services for refugees in the United States.

Looking at the Data: Public Assistance and Welfare[3]

- The Supplemental Nutrition Assistance Project (SNAP) is a federal program that is administered at the local and state level. It was formerly known as "food stamps" and it "helps low-income people buy nutritious food."[4]
- SNAP is for citizens and noncitizens, but the latter wait five years to be SNAP eligible. There are some groups, including refugees, who are exempt from this requirement.[5]
- Between 2005 and 2014, 21 percent of refugees used SNAP versus 15 percent of the U.S. population as a whole.[6]
- But only 2.3 percent of refugees were eligible for Temporary Assistance for Needy Families (TANF), which is a federal cash-aid program.[7]
- In the 2018 fiscal year, 40.8 million Americans, on average, received SNAP monthly at a yearly cost of $60.9 billion.[8]
- 60 percent of SNAP recipients in 2018 were noncitizens.[9]

---

3. We want readers to know that even though refugees depend on government assistance, there are few publicly available statistics of how many refugees are enrolled in SNAP and other programs. This makes it challenging to provide a clear picture of the levels of welfare dependence in the United States. Taking this a step further, we suggest that the lack of accurate data is a contributing factor to some of the prevailing attitudes about refugees and how much support should be provided in the long- and short term.

4. Social Security Administration. 2019. "Supplemental Nutrition Assistance Program (SNAP) Facts." https://www.ssa.gov/pubs/EN-05-10101.pdf

5. Ibid.

6. Madeline Buiano, and Susan Ferriss. 2019. "Data Defies Trump's Claims That Refugees and Asylees Burden Taxpayers." The Center for Public Integrity (Immigration), May 8. https://publicintegrity.org/inequality-poverty-opportunity/immigration/data-defies-trump-claims-that-refugees-and-asylees-are-a-taxpayer-burden/

7. Ibid.

8. Sarah Lauffer, and Alma Vigil. 2021. "Trends in Supplemental Nutrition Assistance Program Participation Rates: Fiscal Year 2016 to Fiscal Year 2018." Prepared by Mathematica for Office of Policy Support, Food and Nutrition Service, United States Department of Agriculture, p. xiii.

9. Ibid, p. 3.

The Question: If refugees face obstacles and challenges even after being accepted and resettled in the United States, why does the federal government allow individual agencies and states to have so many different policies? Why not create one, national standard of refugee care?

Learning Objectives

Reading this chapter will enable readers to:

- **Explain** how the pressure to integrate and be self-sufficient can hurt refugees and cause more trauma.
- **Question** the inadequate level of housing many refugees continue to receive and how that is a form of de facto segregation.
- **Demonstrate** knowledge of community-based organizations and how they build trust and meet the needs of refugees.

Figure 7.1   Family and friends gather to celebrate during a naturalization ceremony.

Staff Sgt. Alexxis Mercer, https://commons.wikimedia.org/wiki/
File:Family,_friends_gather_to_celebrate_during_naturalization_ceremony_150320-F-YG475-377.jpg, 2019.

Pressure to Resettle

As a product of eviscerated funding mechanisms and federal law governing resettlement, on average, refugees are eligible for agency-provided services during their first three months in the U.S. through their 12th month; only some refugees are eligible for services up to a maximum of five years. Refugees' first three months of support is referred to as Reception and Placement,[10] including one-time cash assistance, and is coordinated through the U.S. Department of State. Support and services after the initial three months are coordinated by the U.S. Department of Health and Human Services's Office of Refugee Resettlement[11] and local agencies.

As we highlighted in Chapter 5, the reality of resettlement is that each state has different criteria for redistributing federal funds related to assistance, aid, and welfare. This can also be complicated by policy structure and implementation, particularly in states where all the resettlement is coordinated by private agencies. The disturbing reality of American immigration history, however, is that not all refugees or displaced people receive the same level of care. According to one political scientist,

> scholars have documented many instances in which groups that were perceived to have more resources, or political support, were given more government assistance … Nowhere has this been revealed with so much disturbing clarity as the government's treatment of refugees from Vietnam, Cambodia, and Laos. This is not just about issues with adjustment and integration; Hmong, Laotian, Cambodian, and Vietnamese refugees have received subpar housing, less monetary assistance, and disinterested caseworkers.[12]

We know, for example, that Soviet Jews escaping Communism and restrictions on religious freedom were welcomed to the United States by Cold War era presidents; Congress even passed the Lautenberg Amendment to give "presumptive refugee status to Jews and members of certain other groups from the former Soviet Union."[13] These Jewish refugees often received enhanced welfare and assistance by the American Jewish community.[14][15]

But the opposite was often true for Southeast Asian refugees who suffered marginalization and neglect.[16] A 1987 *Washington Post* article remarked that "the plight of the Indochinese is so stark, and so little reported, that numbers illustrating their dependency often provoke disbelief … A staggering 69 percent are on relief." The author noted that at the time in Fresno, California, Hmong refugees from Laos were less than five percent of the county's population, but their welfare consumed one fifth of the county budget.[17] Cambodian refugees who resettled in

10. https://www.state.gov/refugee-admissions/reception-and-placement/

11. https://www.acf.hhs.gov/orr

12. Shyam Sriram. 2018. "The Politics of Refugee Resettlement." PhD Dissertation, University of California Santa Barbara, p. 10.

13. Victor Rosenberg. 2015. "Refugee Status for Soviet Jewish Immigrants to the United States." Touro Law Review, 19 (2): 419–450, p. 420.

14. Steven James Gold. 1992. Refugee Communities: A Comparative Field Study. Vol. 4. Thousand Oaks, Calif.: Sage Publications, Inc.

15. Steven James Gold. 1994. "Soviet Jews in the United States." In The American Jewish Year Book 94: 3–57.

16. Jeremy Hein. 2006. Ethnic Origins: The Adaptation of Cambodian and Hmong Refugees in Four American Cities. New York: Russell Sage Foundation.

17. David Whitman. 1987. "Asian Un-Success Stories." *The Washington Post*, December 27. https://www.washingtonpost.com/archive/opinions/1987/12/27/asian-un-success-stories/c1b2b95a-3e73-45b5-b846-4b1828309781/

the Bronx in the 1980s were essentially forgotten by the federal government, the State of New York, and the city. They were told that welfare would be temporary until they transitioned into real jobs, but that employment never materialized, and the caseworkers' promises were essentially lies.[18] According to one sociologist,

> The [Cambodian] youth I worked with spoke of the indignities of poverty, the anonymity of new immigrant life, and the street violence that kept many of them in a constant state of fear. They lived in apartments that were borderline uninhabitable, and their lives were marked by routine trips to local welfare offices, where they watched bureaucrats humiliate their parents."[19]

Self-sufficiency is frequently the top referenced concept refugees name during this short timeline for resettlement support that overlaps with the challenges to integration, often to the detriment of building friendly, supportive networks and becoming at ease in places of resettlement. In other words, there is so much pressure on refugees to "make it" and be successful that it takes away from the time often needed to create positive and warm relationships with their neighbors. This, in turn, squeezes refugees to assimilate/integrate too quickly, which can affect their attachment to their new society and cause other problems. It also leads to refugees being placed in high-risk, low-wage employment situations, creating a new underclass in society that is forever dependent on welfare and the government.

Over the last twenty years, for example, refugees have increasingly become essential to American poultry and cattle slaughtering and processing plants. According to the Organization for Competitive Markets, a national interest group,

> Mexicans and Guatemalans stand beside workers from Somalia and Myanmar, the Marshall Islands and Palau, on meat and poultry lines from Kansas and Nebraska to Iowa and Missouri to Delaware and Maryland. These workers do much more than make our meat; they and their families have also transformed and revitalized towns across rural America.[20]

Most accounts of refugee work in animal processing, however, paint a less pleasant and more worrisome picture. While refugees often move to new cities and towns seeking work after an initial period of living in the first place of resettlement—a phenomenon known as secondary migration—the pastoral revitalization depicted above is often not experienced by the refugees themselves. Rather, it is "Go there, come back, go to sleep," as one former refugee described it. It is "butchering parts of 3,000 cows per eight-hour shift, a supervisor standing right behind him, using the knife so furiously he would sometimes feel like his ribs were shaking loose."[21]

18. Eric Tang. 2015. Unsettled: Cambodian Refugees in the New York City Hyperghetto. Philadelphia: Temple University Press, p. 81.
19. Ibid, p. 7.
20. Don Stull. 2017. "Refugees, Meatpacking, and Rural Communities." Organization for Competitive Markets, March 18. https://competitivemarkets.com/refugees-meatpacking-and-rural-communities/
21. Chico Harlan. 2016. "For Somalis, Hope Falls to the Cutting Floor." The Washington Post, May 24. https://www.washingtonpost.com/sf/national/2016/05/24/for-many-somali-refugees-this-industry-offers-hope-then-takes-it-away/?tid=usw_passupdatepg

Looking at the Legislative Language on Self-Sufficiency

- Refugee resettlement is codified, or made part of federal law, through the 1980 Refugee Act and the Electronic Code of Federal Regulations (eCFR).
- Title 45, §400.1 (b) and (c) of the eCFR states the primary motivation behind the refugee resettlement program is "to achieve economic self-sufficiency as quickly as possible" and "the provision of employment services and English language training as a priority in accomplishing the purpose of this program."[22]
- Self-sufficiency is established in the U.S. Refugee Act (1980) through: "sufficient resources for employment training and placement in order to achieve economic self-sufficiency among refugees as quickly as possible … provide refugees with the opportunity to acquire sufficient English language training to enable them to become effectively resettled as quickly as possible … insure [sic] that cash assistance is made available to refugees in such a manner as not to discourage their economic self-sufficiency" (Sec. 411. [8 U.S.C. 1521] paras. 7, 8, 9).
- Section B of the Refugee Act (1980) additionally states Congress's intent for U.S. resettled refugees to "be placed on jobs as soon as possible after their arrival in the United States" (Sec. 411. [8 U.S.C. 1521], para. 12).

Groups that work with or serve refugees often talk about self-sufficiency as if it is a uniform concept with uniform applications. A common belief is that self-sufficiency is synonymous with successful integration into U.S. society primarily achieved through adults' employment and children's school enrollment; items, such as friendship and basic education, like cultural orientation for adults takes a secondary placement if addressed at all. It is not unusual to encounter the belief that self-sufficiency is an unquestionably good goal for refugees. The underbelly of this idea, though, is an assimilationist belief that hard work and determination are enough to overcome the systemic and overlapping challenges of resettlement. For example, how many Americans are aware that refugees must pay their resettlement agencies back for the airfare costs to reach the United States?[23] Assimilationist beliefs manifest as a de facto emphasis on individualism[24] regardless of refugees' cultural backgrounds that may instead center collectivism. Assimilation assumes refugees should abandon all cultural aspects of their identities in lieu of an unobtainable and mythologized Americanness.

22. https://www.ecfr.gov/current/title-45/subtitle-B/chapter-IV/part-400.

23. Molly Fee. 2023. "'Resettled into Poverty:' Structural Violence, Trauma, and the Labor Market Incorporation of Refugees Into the United States." Working Paper.

24. Samuel Bazzie, Martin Fiszbein, and Mesay Gebresilasse. 2020. "Frontier culture: The roots and persistence of 'rugged individualism' in the United States." Econometrica 88 (6): 2329–68. https://doi.org/10.3982/ECTA16484

On the surface, employment is positive because it provides a source of money; sometimes benefits, like health insurance; and workplace interactions with local people, who can informally help refugees understand and acclimate to U.S. and local cultures. From an economic perspective, becoming employed positively contributes to refugees' regaining control over their lives. Forced migration frequently involves refugees being recipients of others' decisions over their lives.[25] For example, in places of temporary resettlement, refugees may not be allowed to work or intermingle with local populations surrounding places of temporary resettlement; also, refugees who are successful in pursuing resettlement do not have a choice in what country they are placed or where they will live once resettled because these decisions are made by the complex of multinational and refugee resettlement agencies. However, employment as the successful achievement of self-sufficiency[26] evidences the one-size-fits-all approach that fails many recently resettled refugees in the U.S. by equating economic participation with full participation.[27]

At a deeper level, much of the working opportunities available to refugees are low wage and high risk, and they tend to offer only a fraction of the surface-level positive aspects. As additional context, refugees are eligible to work in the U.S. from their first day of arrival through a form called the "I-9 for work authorization."[28] However, eligibility is not synonymous with equitable economic participation, which the organizations Asylum Access, the Center for Global Development (CGD), and Refugees International addressed in a 2022 report titled "The Global Refugee Work Rights Scorecard," addressing both de facto and de jure employment rights.[29] The U.S. earned a four out of five in both categories.[30] Additionally, many refugees do not start working from day one and instead pursue employment after participating in an Office of Refugee Resettlement-funded employment program. Based on 2014 data, ORR reported the number of refugees participating in their employment programs and rates of job placements: in North Carolina, the seventh highest destination for U.S.-resettled refugees in 2018,[31] 1,744 refugees participated in employment programs, and 88% of those were placed in jobs.[32] ORR did not report refugees' job placement industries. The American Immigration Council (AIC), though, does feature detailed industry data by state, and these data unfortunately include all types of immigrants. To continue with the example of North Carolina, AIC reported that in 2018, "548,197 immigrant workers comprised 11 percent of the labor force"[33] and that immigrants

25. C. Clark-Kazak, and M. J. Thomson. (2019). "Refugees' roles in resettlement from Uganda and Tanzania: Agency, intersectionality, and relationships." In M. Bradley, J. Milner, and B. Peruniak (Eds.) Refugees' roles in resolving displacement and building peace: Beyond beneficiaries (pp. 211–228). Georgetown University Press. https://www.jstor.org/stable/j.ctvfrxq90.16

26. Heba Gowayed. 2022. Refuge: How the state shapes human potential. Oxford: Princeton University Press.

27. T. A. Dykstra-Devette. 2018. "Resettlement rhetoric: Challenging neoliberalism in refugee empowerment initiatives." *Southern Communication Journal*, 83(3), 179–191. http://doi.org/10.1080/1041794X.2018.1437925

28. https://www.uscis.gov/i-9-central/asylees-and-refugees

29. https://refugeeworkrights.org/scorecard/

30. The Global Refugee Work Rights Scorecard described a four rating for de jure as "There are national policies, but they limit full access to work rights, there are bureaucratic barriers that make the process onerous and/or untimely for livelihood purposes, and/or many labor protections are not extended to refugees" and a four rating for de facto as "Refugees face some discrimination from government officials in accessing employment or other barriers to their right to work in practice."

31. https://immigrationforum.org/article/fact-sheet-u-s-refugee-resettlement/

32. https://www.acf.hhs.gov/orr/grant-funding/fiscal-year-2014-refugee-employment-entered-rates

33. https://www.americanimmigrationcouncil.org/research/immigrants-north-carolina

were numerous in industries of manufacturing, construction, accommodation and food services, health care and social assistance, and the retail trade.

Refugees placed in openings in manufacturing and food processing corporations will experience physically dangerous working conditions where injuries are likely, intense noise that prevents conversation or connection with other workers, and the possibility of long commutes or shifts that conflict with normal business hours. This last point, especially, prevents access to agency, medical, educational, and public-service offerings during these business hours that are vital for refugees' whole-person health and well-being. Additionally, the mental and emotional toll of employment in grueling working conditions lead to a sense of isolation and diminished self-concept that can cause anxiety and depression, further limiting refugees' energy and capacity for attending to multiple pathways toward successful integration. This has been termed "integration distress" or "a general malaise and loss of confidence in not only the U.S., but also in the resettlement process, individual RROs, and their staff … [refugees] felt frustration, sadness, depression, vulnerability, and lack of efficacy about their futures in this country."[34]

Agencies' working cultures are foundational to refugees' early resettlement experiences. Through their role in supporting refugees' transition from places of temporary to long-term resettlement, agencies are vital in establishing refugees' initial and baseline understandings of the local context and culture, as well as refugees' rights and responsibilities; agencies become primary authorities for refugees in the early stages of resettlement from their first days through the first year.[35] From a governmental level, refugees' obligations are described in vague terms that do not explicitly define "self-sufficiency" or "sufficient" education and training; thus, agencies that work at the local level are left to interpret and apply these vague terms with refugee clients. Local contexts and beliefs about refugees additionally influence how agencies understand refugee law and convey it to clients.[36]

In the first chapter of this textbook, we discussed how U.S. federal policy and funding mechanisms for refugee resettlement admissions and support have been drastically cut over recent years as a byproduct of anti-immigrant sentiment.[37] Less funding resulted in some agencies closing and others drastically reducing their staff; in both cases, refugees suffer the consequences of less accessible support personnel and increased isolation.[38] By contrast, the culture of community-based organizations (CBOs) is also vital in humanizing how refugees understand and navigate their places of resettlement, which is covered in greater detail in subsequent sections.

34. Shyam K. Sriram. 2020. "Of Acculturative Stress and Integration Distress: The Resettlement Challenges of Bhutanese Refugees in Metro Atlanta." *South Asian Diaspora* 12 (1): 93–108.

35. Cathryn B. Bennett. 2022. "Refugee Women and Higher Education Across Space, Place, and Time." PhD Dissertation, University of North Carolina at Greensboro.

36. Stacey A. Shaw, Mallory Funk, Elisabeth Schaerr Garlock, and Adhieu Arok. 2021. "Understanding Successful Refugee Resettlement in the U.S." *Journal of Refugee Studies*, 34 (4): 4034–4052. https://doi.org/10.1093/jrs/feaa137

37. Bobby Allyn. 2019. "Trump Administration Drastically Cuts Number of Refugees Allowed to Enter the U.S." National Public Radio: All Things Considered, September 26. https://www.npr.org/2019/09/26/764839236/trump-administration-drastically-cuts-numberof-refugees-allowed-to-enter-the-u

38. Tania Karas. 2019. "US Refugee Agencies Wither as Trump Administration Cuts Numbers to Historic Low." PRI (The World), September 27. https://www.pri.org/stories/2019-09-27/us-refugee-agencieswither-trump-administration-cuts-numbers-historic-lows

Inadequate Housing

Housing is another essential feature of how agencies shape integration, especially in the early period of time for post-resettled refugees. Agencies decide where refugees will live upon resettlement, and this practice is frequently referred to as "placement" services.[39] Unfortunately, viable or affordable housing options must fall within the preset range of refugees' housing credit. Cheap apartments tend to be outside city centers: de facto segregation is another outcome of this reality. Much of the U.S. is notorious for poor infrastructure for public transit options. Affordable apartments in fringe neighborhoods away from city centers, combined with unreliable public transportation, makes inaccessible vital public spaces and services. Also, places like libraries, parks, governmental offices, and even agency offices are, by default, challenging to reach. These dynamics effectively segregate refugees from other populations and threaten successful integration into local communities.

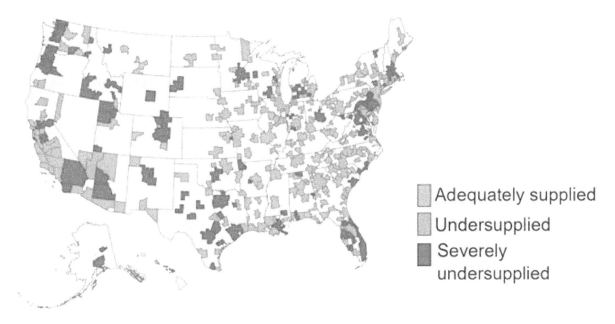

Adequately supplied
Undersupplied
Severely undersupplied

Figure 7.2   National Housing Shortage. source=Moody's Analytics, https://www.weforum.org/agenda/2022/06/how-to-fix-global-housing-crisis/. Copyright © 2022 by Moody's Analytics, Inc.

The lack of quality housing for refugees is part of a much larger problem about lack of affordable housing nationally [see Figure 7.2]. Refugees and those seeking asylum in the United States—who are in the process of applying for permanent residence but are in bureaucratic limbo—are often resettled in cities, towns, and states that already suffer from housing shortages. This not only denies refugees the fundamental right to safe housing

39. Silvia Mathema, and Sofia Carratala. 2020. "Rebuilding the U.S. Refugee Program for the 21st Century." American Progress, October 26. https://www.americanprogress.org/issues/immigration/reports/2020/10/26/492342/rebuilding-u-s-refugee-program-21st-century/

guaranteed by national and international law[40] but makes it harder for refugees to integrate into communities because locals may resent the arrival of these newcomers. An oft-repeated story that illustrates this very point goes back to 1981 and a confrontation resulting in death between white and Vietnamese fishermen in Texas after thousands of Vietnamese refugees were relocated to Texas following the Vietnam War, often into communities already facing economic hardship.[41] There was so much tension that according to one account, "on March 15 [1981], the Ku Klux Klan and Texas militia groups paraded past working Vietnamese-owned shrimp boats, wearing menacing robes and hoods, and waving firearms in the air."[42]

As Figure 7.2 illustrates, there are large swathes of the country that have little housing available, particularly in urban areas but also in rural communities, as well. Refugees and asylum seekers arriving from South and Central America may need to travel north to find adequate housing, as southern states like California, Nevada, Texas, and Florida have concentrated shortages, particularly in the lower halves of the states. As shown, housing is scarce for individuals and families arriving or traveling to the western United States, save for parts of California. It's important to also note that these shortages affect residents as well as refugees and asylum seekers; influxes of immigrants to areas noted to be severely undersupplied may lead to tension between the immigrants and the established population.

More recently, for example, Governor Kevin Stitt of Oklahoma agreed to accept over 1,800 humanitarian evacuees from Afghanistan between 2021 and 2022 even though resettlement organizations knew there was insufficient housing. Some of these Afghani evacuees served honorably with U.S. military forces and then found themselves in deplorable apartments in Oklahoma that included everything from cockroach infestations and zero air-conditioning to broken windows and perpetually clogged drains.[43] In a somewhat similar tale of woe, according to an account of a family from Afghanistan who received emergency placement in California:

> From the airport, they were transported to a mosque near Union City, where they slept on floor mats for one night, shielded by a single curtain. Without any money to spend on Ubers or bus passes, the family walked an hour and 40 minutes to a local nonprofit, the Afghan Coalition, to begin the process of resettlement.[44]

Resettlement under these dire housing and living circumstances can be especially dangerous for refugees, as we discussed in the last section on self-sufficiency, because they are seen as competition for housing and jobs even though refugees and recent immigrants often take the least-skilled and dangerous jobs that other Americans do not want. Imagine a scenario where your family is resettled in Massachusetts, the state with the second highest cost of

40. Joel Glasman. 2020. Humanitarianism and the Quantification of Human Needs: Minimal Humanity. (Ser. Routledge humanitarian studies). Routledge. https://www.taylorfrancis.com/books/9781003006954

41. https://www.npr.org/2022/08/01/1114451029/how-white-nationalists-in-texas-terrorized-refugees-after-the-vietnam-war

42. Houston Institute for Culture. 2017."The Asian American Experience: Building New Saigon." http://www.houstonculture.org/cultures/viet.html

43. Lionel Ramos. 2022. "Why Some Afghan Refugees in State Live in Squalor." Oklahoma Watch, September 3. https://www.normantranscript.com/news/why-some-afghan-refugees-in-state-live-in-squalor/article_fa51c458-2aff-11ed-b0a6-a3dae5821883.html

44. Makena Kelly. 2022. "Unsettled: The Afghan Refugee Crisis Collides With the American Housing Disaster." The Verge, June 29. https://www.theverge.com/c/23170906/homeland-unsettled-afghan-refugee-crisis-housing-bay-area

living in the United States.[45] A few of your family members know some English but not enough to ask for a better place to live. Back in Afghanistan, your family has a distinct military heritage, and you lived a comfortable life. Now, five sisters, your parents, and you live in a two-bedroom, poorly insulated apartment, and share one bathroom. Who do you ask for help?

Agency dependence on low-rent housing also has far more materially damaging consequences than isolation. For example, in 2018 in Greensboro, North Carolina, tragedy struck a recently resettled refugee family as a direct consequence of placement in low rent but unsafe housing. Five children died in an entirely preventable house fire; they were all under the age of 8 years old.[46] The property owner knew of the malfunctioning stove in the family's apartment yet chose to not make repairs in a display of flagrant and willful ignorance. The agency that was meant to facilitate the integration of this refugee family from the Democratic Republic of the Congo (DRC) into American society placed them in this apartment complex for its affordability without consideration of the numerous reports from other refugees already residing there of the landlord's irresponsible attitude toward bare minimum requirements of safe and hygienic housing. In this situation, inadequate housing simultaneously reproduced de facto segregation, grief, and trauma that reverberated throughout the refugee communities in the area.[47]

Solutions to Resettlement and Integration Crises

Unlike agencies, community-based organizations (CBOs) are not required to only offer refugee services according to the amount of time since being resettled. Instead, CBOs frequently operate through a culture of humanization and relationship-building and are less likely than agencies to offer time-bound services. Importantly, CBOs do not follow a uniform set of practices throughout the U.S. but, instead, tend to formulate their working practices in direct connection to local communities. However, CBOs tend to rely on practices involving the requisite time needed to build connections with refugee clients predicated on trust.

Community "groundedness," or commitments to addressing local community needs through education and services, is an essential feature of how CBOs work with refugee clients. While certainly informed by national level law, policy, and beliefs, CBOs' close proximity to local communities provide a locus of control that is more responsive to community-level realities. For example, CBOs outside metropolitan areas with robust public transport may provide free bus or train vouchers for refugee clients to be able to access their locations. Additionally, CBOs center refugees in their services also balance this with presence in the community to educate and inform nonrefugees about their experiences. Nonrefugee community members tend to be surprised when learning some of the basic distinctions among classifications like immigrant, migrant, and refugee, for example.

Extended time—beyond the limits of agency services—affords refugees conceptual space to acclimate gently and in contrast to the outside pressures of forced integration. Unlike agencies, CBOs are not required to operate

45. Missouri Economic Research and Information Center. 2022. "2022 Third Quarter Cost of Living." https://meric.mo.gov/data/cost-living-data-series

46. David Ford. 2018. "Chapter 1: The Fatal Fire." Unsafe Haven (WFDD). https://www.wfdd.org/story/chapter-1-fatal-fire

47. Amanda Magnus, and Frank Stasio. 2018. "How a Deadly Fire Laid Bare Housing Issues in Greensboro." WUNC 91.5, North Carolina Public Radio (December 11). https://www.wunc.org/race-demographics/2018-12-11/how-a-deadly-fire-laid-bare-housing-issues-in-greensboro

on the three- to 12-month time limit for services offered. Instead, CBOs support refugees based on their personal development and evolving needs. This may look like supporting a refugee who wishes to retake an English class to build their confidence or being available to answer questions about lease renewals or taxes well after the period of their first-year post-resettlement. CBOs approach to availability over an extended period of time conveys consistency and reliability.

The combination of CBOs as embedded in their local communities and the absence of time pressures for refugees to perform integration leads to enhanced trust. Developing trust between refugees and those who work with them affords better insights into refugees' lives, skills, and the knowledge or tools needed for them to create good lives on their *own terms*. This is in direct opposition to the one-size-fits-all model of federally funded agencies where employment is synonymous with success. Thus, CBOs offer lasting and humanizing solutions to facilitate refugee integration.

The effect of these practices for how CBOs work with refugees is essential. Notably, as we discussed at the beginning of this textbook, refugees do not electively move from their homes; they are forced to migrate.[48] Through forced migration experiences, refugees are additionally forced to follow laws, regulations, and customs that are not familiar or their own: collectively, these experiences can erode refugees' expressions of agency and self-concepts. While agencies are legally bound to only a certain level and type of service provisions, CBOs instead develop relationships with refugees that are based on reciprocity and responsiveness that seek to reprioritize refugees' own desires and intentions for their lives post-resettlement. Agencies' relationships with refugees demonstrate a one-way transmission of power and knowledge *onto* refugees while CBOs work *with* refugees to express and use their collective community power.[49] The following examples of noteworthy CBOs demonstrate effective working relationships *with* refugees.

Every Campus A Refuge (ECAR) is one laudable example of a CBO approach in the resettlement landscape. Dr. Diya Abdo started ECAR on Guilford College's campus to ease refugees' initial transitions into the U.S. The ECAR model supports colleges and universities in becoming resettlement campuses. This entails offering rent-free, on-campus housing and access to the established community of campuses and the surrounding area.[50] ECAR does not supplant but rather supplements agency support; a local resettlement agency provides legally required support while ECAR fills in the gaps of community and consistency. Additionally, since refugees housed through ECAR do not pay rent, the portion of funds all refugees receive to subsidize housing is saved until they move out of the ECAR-sponsored housing. Importantly, ECAR reinforces refugees' empowerment by supporting them with finding safe and affordable housing and not rushing their transition from ECAR housing to another home.

Another example of a refugee-focused CBO is Tapestri in Tucker, Georgia. What makes Tapestri unique is that it is one of very few community organizations aimed at helping victims of intimate partner violence who are

48. UNHCR refugee definition.

49. Delma Ramos, and M. Sarubbi. 2021. "Conceptualizations of power & agency among members of refugee communities in the state of Colorado." New Directions for Higher Education, 2020, 31–41. https://doi.org/10.1002/he.20380

50. Diya Abdo, and Krista Craven. 2018. "Every Campus a Refuge: A Small College's Engagement with Refugee Resettlement." Migration and Society 1 (1): 135–146.

refugees and immigrants. The community-based organization offers everything from counseling, interpreting, and legal counseling to trainings on human trafficking and support for unaccompanied minors. According to their vision,

> We do not see domestic violence, sexual assault, and exploitation as the problem of an individual, couple, or even one particular community, but rather, a human rights issue. It is a phenomenon perpetuated in societies in which gender inequality and violence are accepted. Tapestri seeks to educate individuals and agencies so that these destructive norms will not continue into the next generation.[51]

The New Arrivals Institute[52] (NAI) in Greensboro, North Carolina, is yet another robust example of a CBO that humanizes refugee resettlement support. NAI works closely with local resettlement agencies to ensure that newly arrived refugees are aware of the broad array of services and supports they offer, including education placement testing and credential evaluation, English and citizenship classes, case management, and health literacy. As a community organization, NAI prioritizes services for refugees and educational community outreach:

> New Arrivals Institute is not only a resource and educational service provider to refugees and immigrants, but also serves as a resource to the community at large about refugees and immigrants and their issues.

This balance between refugee service provisions and community outreach and education evidence NAI's community-centered approach. One particularly humanizing element of NAI practice pertains specifically to women's and caretakers' empowerment: NAI offers free childcare for any client who comes in for classes or an appointment. They also offer free bus passes to support access. Furthermore, they do not require clients to stop receiving services at any particular period of time; this affords ongoing trust and relationship-building that productively works *with* refugees as they rebuild their lives post-resettlement.

List of Key Takeaways

Review the list of bullet points below for a quick overview of the key ideas and information in this chapter:

- Refugees face an enormous amount of stress and urgency to integrate into the United States after arriving in this country.
- This is partly due to vague standards and ideas of self-sufficiency maintained by the federal and state governments.
- Much of that pressure, however, comes from refugee resettlement organizations (RROs), but their services are often inadequate to meet all their clients' needs. Community-based organizations (CBOs) often provide services to fill the gaps.

51. https://tapestri.org/at-a-glance/
52. The New Arrivals Institute. 2018. https://newarrivalsinstitute.org/

- Examples of CBOs include Every Campus a Refuge (ECAR) and the New Arrivals Institute (NAI), both based in North Carolina.
- One historic and well-known problem is that Southeast Asian refugees have often received fewer public and private resources compared to other comparable groups.
- Refugees must enter the workforce immediately but often end up in manufacturing and animal processing jobs despite having higher qualifications than many native-born workers.
- One of the unseen challenges facing refugees is finding good quality and clean housing. But there is a national housing shortage that overlaps with resettlement sites; refugees are often placed in towns and cities that already have a dearth of safe housing.
- Most refugees are heavily dependent on public assistance programs like SNAP and often are more reliant than native-born populations.

Chapter Review Questions

1. **What** is another name for the first three months of resettlement?
   a. Advanced Placement
   b. Reception and Placement (CORRECT)
   c. Revise and Resubmit
   d. Rest and Relaxation
2. After rereading the opening vignette, **what** do you recall as the number one challenge for Rosie and her family?
3. **Explain** the phenomenon of secondary migration.
4. **Provide** at least ONE disadvantage associated with the definition of assimilation. Why is assimilation a poor explanation for refugees' lived experiences?
5. Compare and **contrast** refugee resettlement organizations (RROs) and community-based organizations (CBOs). What is one primary difference?
6. **How** might Tapestri's approach to intimate partner violence help refugees more than agencies that do not typically work with displaced people?

Critical Thinking Prompts

1. **Interpret** this statement: "Extended time—beyond the limits of agency services—affords refugees conceptual space to acclimate gently and in contrast to the outside pressures of forced integration." Why would agencies have "limits"? What is "conceptual space"?

2. **Discuss** the 2018 apartment fire in Greensboro, North Carolina. How did that tragedy illustrate the dilemma of proper resettlement policy and implementation?

3. **Formulate** THREE solutions for resettlement agencies to alleviate integration-related challenges for refugees.

4. In your own words, **disprove** the idea that refugees who receive immediate authorization to work actually benefit from this employment.

Milton Keynes UK
Ingram Content Group UK Ltd.
UKHW030623010824
446326UK00007B/266

9 781793 588326